HARRY'S BAR

Also by Arrigo Cipriani

Heloise and Bellinis

HARRY'S BAR

The Life and Times of the
Legendary Venice Landmark

Arrigo Cipriani

ARCADE PUBLISHING • NEW YORK

FIRST EDITION

The photographs on the third page of the photo insert showing the front window and entrance of Harry's Bar are by Denholm Jacobs III.

Library of Congress Cataloging-in-Publication Data

Cipriani, Arrigo
    Harry's Bar : the life and times of the legendary Venice land-
mark / Harry Cipriani.
        p.   cm.
    ISBN-13: 978-1-55970-259-1
    ISBN 10: 1-55970-259-1
    1. Harry's Bar (Venice, Italy) — History.   2. Cookery, Italian.
3. Celebrities — Social life and customs.
TX945.5.H37C55   1996
641.5'0945'31 — dc20   95-53077

Published in the United States by Arcade Publishing, Inc., New York
Distributed by Hachette Book Group USA

10 9 8

EB

Designed by API

PRINTED IN THE UNITED STATES OF AMERICA

CONTENTS

SERVICE

There is soul, and there are things.
Imagine a world made up only of objects,
A world of idle tools,
A restaurant of nothing but tables and chairs,
A large empty theater, or a deserted plaza in summer.
They cry out for the service of man,
The service to give them life.
We call on man to display his splendid capabilities.
And
We observe with undivided attention,
Because
The little nuances in the quality of his service
Give a flawless measure of his mind,
They tell us frankly what his soul is worth,
Because,
To serve is first to love.

HARRY'S BAR

INTRODUCTION

ONE VERY MUGGY SUMMER DAY in the late 1960s, I went to see my father in his home in the Valsugana Mountains near Trento, where in his later years he sometimes took a month's vacation. I had been running Harry's Bar for a little over ten years, and, in theory at least, my father was no longer involved in the day-to-day business of the bar he had founded in 1931 and built up to the legendary Venice restaurant it had become. Of course, until the day he died, my father would never accept that he was no longer in charge of Harry's Bar — and a good thing it was, too. My father *was* Harry's Bar. Had he ever really broken all connections with the restaurant, he would have ceased to exist. After he "retired" from managing Harry's Bar, he still came every day for lunch and was always our most demanding customer — the one

1

we tried most to please, and the one who was most sparing with his approval. But a good word from him meant more than all the lavish praise we got from our real customers.

I didn't arrive at Trento until the afternoon, later than I had planned. My father came toward me with that slightly hurried step of his, and he could not refrain from scolding me for my tardiness. I expected that, of course. In the twenty years I ran Harry's Bar while he was alive, I don't think I was late for work a single time. Getting to work by ten o'clock in the morning and again at six for the evening meal was like a law of nature in our family, and I'm sure that if anyone had ever asked me I would have said that the world would end if I ever arrived for work as much as a minute late. Today, I sometimes think that the strict adherence to a daily routine that I learned from my father, as useful as it is, ruined my taste for discipline forever. For example, soon after he died, I developed an immediate distaste for getting to appointments on time, even for scheduling appointments at all, and it's an aversion that has never left me.

That summer day, my father greeted me heartily, then hurried off to the warmest room in the house to see if the *Krapfen* dough was rising. As everyone in the family knew, fritters had always been my favorite sweet. A moment later he reappeared disgruntled, because the dough had risen too much. As usual, he asked how business had been going while he was away, but this time he did not pay much attention to what I said. He was clearly following his own train of thought elsewhere. We were sitting on the shady side of the house, on a terrace overlooking the meadow, and he suddenly started to talk about Germany, where he had spent his childhood, and about German lieder. And then he started to sing, softly. The lied spoke of an exile's nostalgia for his home in Spain and his all-consuming longing to return.

It was then I discovered a side to my father I had never seen before, and I was glad, because only our family knows how little of it we saw when he was alive. Never had he told me in any explicit way whether I lived up to the expectations he had for the heir to the family business. But on that summer afternoon, I began to realize that I knew him more from what he did over the course of his life than from what he said.

Many of the episodes described in the first part of this book, as told by my father, were events I witnessed too; others he told me about; and still others are part of our family heritage — Mama Giulia, my mother, told them to the three of us when we were children. We listened eagerly, as children do to old stories about the grown-ups, as she told them in the evening, while we were alone, and he was at work.

1

GIUSEPPE

The first part of the book is told in the first person by
my father, Giuseppe Cipriani, the founder of Harry's Bar in
Venice.

One morning in 1970 as I was signing some papers at my
lawyer's office, my right hand suddenly felt very light:
the more I tried to hold it down, the more it wanted to
rise, as if it had become totally weightless. At the moment it happened, I was rather amused by this strange
sensation, and I was far from imagining what it really was.
They told me later in the hospital: paralysis.

That was the morning old age hit me. I understood for the first time what it was like to feel tired even
after a good night's sleep. It was then I first began very
slowly to look back at the past and review the events,

the people, and the situations that I had experienced in all those long years since I founded Harry's Bar, and during the time before. The older one gets, the more vivid childhood episodes become, events that are remote in time yet so close in memory you can almost touch them.

My family came from Verona. My father worked as a porter and wore himself out for eighty centesimi a day. He had eight children to support, four boys and four girls.

Those were the years when Italians could obtain the so-called red passport and cross the Atlantic to the United States, jammed into the ships of the Rubattino line. My father in Verona looked for a haven nearer home: Germany.

In 1904 we arrived in Schwenningen am Neckar. My family felt at home at once. The climate and the hilly landscape on the banks of the river were rather similar to those of Verona. And several of our neighbors from Verona were already there, so we settled in easily.

The Germans called us *Itakas*. They were slow to accept us, but they understood that we meant well. They blew off steam mainly with harmless jokes about Italians that for the most part put us in a good humor too.

Like most of his countrymen who ended up in those parts, my father worked as a bricklayer. He made twenty-three marks per week — the equivalent of two hundred dollars today — which was five times what he had earned in Italy.

My mother also did her share to keep things going in the little house we rented. She took in boarders: room, *Frühstück*, and, of course, a liter of beer a day, all for one mark fifty. I may have been drawn to the calling of barman and hotelier (I ought to be more modest and say taverner or saloonkeeper) by watching my mother deal with our roomers. She was kind and considerate, but not servile. That is a hard balance to strike, as I can testify today after years of experience myself.

We children went to school. It took us about a year to become fairly fluent in the language. We made friends with German children, chiefly children of day laborers and factory workers like us, since Schwenningen had many factories by then. Looking back on it now, it was a good life for us children, especially for me. If we had stayed in Italy, it would have been very hard to go to school and learn something.

Today I can say without any ambivalent feelings: I grew up German, and I felt German. I was perfectly at home in that environment and identified with that cleanliness and order, a discipline that was so wise and, at that time, so far from being exploited by a fanatic like Hitler. I felt I was a German, and a good German. I was proud to live in a country where education was free and where, at the end of elementary school, students were carefully evaluated and advised on what direction to take in life. The year after a boy finished school, he might go to work as an apprentice in a factory or in some artisan's shop.

With pay and insurance, naturally. Even if he was a foreigner. For immigrants like us, all this meant an end to our former poverty.

After eight years of elementary school, my teachers suggested that I continue my studies at a *Gymnasium*, the secondary school for pupils destined to go to university. Unfortunately we did not have enough money at the time, so I became a helper in a watch factory. I now see clearly how big a part this first job played in forming my character: the sense of precision, the love of order, and the aversion for things not done properly that I have always had. They all came to me there among the gears and hairsprings.

The outbreak of World War I in 1914 put an end to my carefree days. It was a tragedy for me. I could not understand why, in the country I loved as my own, everyone — those who had taken care of me and my family, my classmates, and all those fine people of Schwenningen — had suddenly become the enemy, people I might have to shoot at. Mistrust of us *"Itakas"* developed slowly, like a nasty illness; and before long, what had been a friendly sounding nickname became a scornful epithet.

So we returned to Verona. I was fourteen years old, and there was no money; but there was work, because the adult men were going off to war. At Molinari's, one of the finest pastry shops in Verona, the owner had almost no one left.

Why did I choose to work in a pastry shop? Maybe because my father had heard there was a job. Yet it was an important choice in my life. I began to put my hands in dough: a man of bars, restaurants, and hotels also needs to have a thorough understanding of the secrets of pastry. Before long, I learned the art of making pastry light as a feather. Meanwhile my father had found work as a helper for another famous pastry maker, Tommasi, who offered me a few centesimi more than I was earning. So, without many second thoughts I brought my recent experience to his shop and resumed manipulating cream puffs.

It was very hard work, but work has never been burdensome to me. On the contrary, I have always enjoyed it. As far back as I can remember, I have been stimulated by the idea of creating something, I have enjoyed making others happy, and I have constantly been driven by a desire to seek something better.

It was still dark when I got up in the morning; not even the street sweepers, who were early risers in those days, were out when I walked to work. There were no set hours: the working day was fifteen, even sixteen hours long. Sometimes we were asleep on our feet, on the verge of collapse, our brains numb and our hands mechanically repeating their task, over and over again: one thousand, one thousand two hundred, one thousand five hundred pastries. When the bells rang out for holidays, it was a real deliverance.

The wood-fired ovens were always open to make sure that the flame, that is to say the heat, was constant. We perspired all the time, even when Christmas snow was falling outside. No electric beaters in those days: egg whites were beaten by hand. It was the simplest work of all, so that was what apprentices, the newcomers, did. I can still see myself during the first months at Tommasi's: the obsession of the production line; the same operation over and over; my right arm spinning at high speed, beating dozens of eggs at a time, and my left hand holding the receptacle firm. Morning to night.

Someone had tossed an old mattress on top of the oven between towers of dough set out for leavening. When we could no longer stand on our feet, we took turns lying on that sort of airborne bed. A couple of quick snores, and then a faint tap on the shoulder. Two bloodshot eyes looked at you, and an exhausted voice would announce the change: "It's my turn."

I earned barely three lire a week. I knew it was nothing, but kneading the dough, doling in the cream, watching the most imaginative forms of pastry come to life, more than made up for the low pay. I would peek out from the workroom at the customers in the shop tasting the fruits of our labor. Giving pleasure to others had become my vocation.

When he went to war, Tommasi turned the shop over to me. I was sixteen years old, and that job lasted about two years, until it occurred to the authorities that pastries were luxury items and banned their production. I will always remember the rush for the last pastries; if we had produced cannons at the same rate as we turned out pastries in those days, we would have won the war in a month.

In 1918 men born in 1900 were also called up, and I left for Sant'Arcangelo di Romagna for basic training. But for me, the war was not something serious, and in that attitude I was not alone. Everything seemed to prevent people from looking martial. At our age, what we thought most about was girls. We would have liked to impress them with our uniforms, but they were almost all hand-me-downs from the dead and wounded. I weighed about 110 pounds, and I made a sorry sight tromping around in old shoes that were three sizes too big for me.

It was an experience, though. I got to know the Italians, and I soon recognized that underneath the disciplined exterior my German childhood had lent me, I was still an Italian myself. When we threw hand grenades during basic training, few of us remembered to pull the pin, and nobody counted to three. I liked that and saw that the difference between us and the Germans was to our credit.

Fortunately, on the eve of departure for the front, my problems of conscience were happily resolved by the armistice. On November 3 we were in Ala, behind the lines; and on November 4, 1918, my eighteenth birthday, the fighting stopped.

Six months of military food, pasta and beans, and long marches did a lot for me physically. I put on more than thirty pounds, and I felt in great form. My mother hardly recognized me when I got back home.

There was a great welcome for me at the pastry shop, but my mania for change, for learning something new, the same mania that had taken me from Molinari's to Tommasi's, took hold of me again. And I decided to become a waiter.

I bought a set of tails and looked good in it: girls looked at me with respect and admiration. I became a "flying" waiter, in the sense that I spun through a whirl of different bars, night spots, trattorias, a kaleidoscope of owners and customers — I was running all the time, almost skating with trays full of orders. I worked at the Gatto Nero, the Torcolo, and the Gabbia d'Oro — in those days one of the best hotels in Verona.

Uppermost in my thoughts, however, were two fixed ideas: to master the craft of restaurateur and to go into business for myself. So I would stay in one place long enough to learn what there was to learn, then I would take off again somewhere else. I would leave one café, and the next day I would be working at the one across the street. My bosses appreciated me for my working so hard, but at the same time they hated me for my faithlessness. That was my way. What I liked most was the constant human contact with the customers. I learned how much people need one another.

But Verona was too small a city. I was already thinking of going away when I was called up again for military service, this time for the ordinary draft. Nothing could have seemed more unfair, and I went to great lengths not to be drafted — no easy matter in those days. For example, to decide if someone were really deaf, he had to walk down a staircase, and they would roll an empty tin garbage can down after him. If he moved out of the way, it proved he was not deaf. If he was hit, he was exempted. I was exempted on the grounds of amblyopia, or lazy eye, which I had actually suffered since birth. It seemed a blessing at the time. Now, with a cataract on my good eye, eyeglasses have become mandatory.

With military service out of the way, I thought that with my experience as a waiter and my perfect knowledge of German, I could get work in a hotel. I boldly answered an advertisement for a *chef de rang* at the Hôtel des Alpes in Madonna di Campiglio. I went with a friend who had the same experience I did — that is to say, next to none, at least as far as hotels were concerned.

The Hôtel des Alpes was magnificent and impressive. It was reopening for the first time after the war, and everything had to be readied and reorganized for the season. After a short interview we were hired on the spot. We opened crates and took out marvelous sets of Limoges porcelain, fine silverware, glistening crystal glasses, and tablecloths of the finest embroidered linen.

All the while, my friend and I were worried because we were practically all alone. There was no maître d', and there was a chef in the kitchen who scared you just to look at him. But he was the only authority we had, so about two weeks before the opening, still a bit awkward in my new tails, I went into the kitchen to talk to him. "Listen, Signor Vismara," I said, "I have to confess that I have never been a hotel waiter before. But I am very anxious to learn, and you must help me."

Vismara had seen how hard I worked getting

the dining room ready, and he replied: "Don't worry, Cipriani, there's nothing to fear. If you have any questions, just come to me."

Vismara was by far the greatest chef I ever met. I have seen a great many, but Vismara remains a shining example of human kindness and simplicity, the simplicity of a man who knows his business. In the rare moments when there was nothing to do, I would go to see him. I would stand at the kitchen door and watch him roll out pastry or bone a lamb. He handled the dough like a sculptor modeling clay, and he approached the lamb as a surgeon would in an operating theater.

Before long, I became his private student. I watched everything he did in silence and committed all his movements to memory. Late at night, before falling asleep, I would repeat his movements in the dark — a kind of mechanical training.

That was the school I grew up in, what they call nowadays the "old school." In the old school, a waiter ran like a locomotive if he wanted to get ahead and one day have a place of his own. Today, there are still a lot of fine young men, but for the most part they fall into one of two categories. There are young people who consider waiting on table a humiliating profession. They take no pleasure in their work, the surest way of staying on the lowest rungs. And then there are excellent but fearful young men afraid to run the risk of going into business on their own.

Getting back to the Hôtel des Alpes in Madonna di Campiglio, the maître d' finally arrived one morning a week before the official opening. He was extremely elegant and had an aristocratic air about him — very solemn, but a bit too silent. He never moved; he would stand in the middle of the room and survey the whole place. But never a comment, no suggestions, and no orders; we never heard him say a word.

Two days before the opening he came over to me and said, "Listen, Cipriani, there's something I ought to tell you. You seem like a bright boy, and you've got to help me." He seemed embarrassed.

"Speak up," I said.

"Well, to tell the truth, I've never been a maître d' before. Can I count on you to help?"

I felt like a lion when I heard that, a real veteran of the profession. "Don't worry," I winked, "we've got everything under control. Count on me for everything!"

After that, it didn't take long before I was made head waiter. This was one year after the war; unemployment was high, and swarms of aspiring waiters appeared every day, people who had never worn a white jacket before. Among my new duties was the job of choosing the new waiters, and I found it was something that came naturally to me. I had a clinical eye for them. I would look a candidate in the eye for half a minute and make up my mind, and I never made a mistake. We began the season like a band of stragglers and ended it like a triumphant army. At the end of the season, the owners made us promise to come back the following year.

After a few stints in Trento at the leading café and very brief stops in Verona, where I had laid eyes on a girl named Giulietta (or maybe she had laid eyes on me), I was off again, from one big hotel to another: from the Meranerhof in Merano to the Hôtel Metropole de Bruxelles at Bagnoles-de-l'Orne in France, then all the way to the Excelsior in Palermo.

In France I learned and understood a great many things aside from the language. What impressed me was not so much the great variety of sauces and combinations of food as the inimitable French art of selling and the importance they gave to color in food. They were absolutely the best at this. The dish that reached the table was as full of color as a beautiful painting, a wonder to look at, even if it was not always wonderful to eat.

And the wines? Splendid, but what contributed to their success in this case was that art of showmanship and that sense of grandeur that is so happily a part of the French character, ever optimistic about life and one's part in it. I admired bottles with marvelous labels in the hands of waiters and sommeliers who treated them with the same care a demolition expert might use with a bomb. Measured, elegant, and respectful gestures gave prestige and nobility to even the simple ritual of drinking a glass of wine. I tasted some of the finest champagnes. They were excellent, but it was all too punctilious. It was almost as if the customers were expected to stop after every sip, bow their heads to the goblet, and whisper thanks! On such occasions, I thought about Italian *spumantes* that did not come in ostentatious bottles but were certainly not inferior to those delicious nectars. I even felt nostalgic for a certain *prosecco* made in the Veneto countryside that was at least a match for a Dom Perignon. Indeed, I later used the humble *prosecco* very successfully in cocktails whose names have become household words around the world.

I felt that there had to be another way of serving people, a way of inspiring the customers' trust without intimidating them, of loving one's guests and not just impressing them. For example, I thought it must be possible to create an elegant atmosphere without the help of the formal, stereotyped flambé. Personally, I have always detested that wordless ritual that customers are expected to watch in ecstasy, and I think those mannered affectations are no substitute for dishes prepared by a loving cook using good and honest ingredients.

After Palermo, finally Venice. It won me over at once with its inimitable human dimension, its great civility, its sudden changes and light, its asymmetry, and the endlessly shifting life of its waters. I found a job at the Monaco, ten feet from a cordage warehouse that would later become Harry's Bar. But I didn't know that yet.

2

AN AMERICAN IN VENICE

MEANWHILE, IN 1926, that girl named Giulietta and I got married. I remember the wedding lunch, where there were more wine bottles than there were guests; and that evening we went to Padua for our honeymoon. The next morning we dashed in and out of what we thought was the Church of Saint Anthony, Padua's patron saint, and headed back to Venice the same day, since I had to return to work the following morning. It was only years later I learned that in our haste that morning we had gone to the wrong church. Saint Anthony, forgive me!

I was still in Venice in 1927, working at the Hotel Europa-Britannia, a beautiful hotel owned by a German family named Walter, and it was Signor Walter who sealed my fate.

"Cipriani," he said one day, "you're going to tend the bar."

"Why?"

"Because you have a way with the customers. They like you, and you know languages." (I had learned English on my own.)

I was not altogether convinced that Signor Walter was right, but I rallied my enthusiasm and became the Europa's barman.

Now, if I speak somewhat nostalgically about the bar at the old Hotel Europa, it is not because I remember that time as the golden age of the gastronomy business, or think that the trade has since gone down the drain. I am not a pessimist. If anyone asks how I am, I always say "fine." If it is a friend who asks, he will be happy to know I am well, and if it is not a friend, the answer will irritate him a bit. I have never been one to say things are going to wrack and ruin, but I do think that everyone seems to have less time nowadays than they did in the past. Everything has to be organized to a prearranged schedule; speed is the keynote of travel, and people live, eat, drink, and even make love with their eyes on the clock.

But in the days when I first started tending bar, the places where people would get together were quiet cafés and hotel bars. A host of people frequented cafés and bars; they sat down together for a drink and relaxed conversation. They were nice times. There were healthy pauses in the course of the day. People set aside more time for themselves, and I think that one day soon they will again feel like sitting down quietly and talking to one another. And perhaps they will want a cocktail to boost their morale.

In those days the Hotel Europa was a meeting place for quite a few young Venetians with time on their hands. They came partly to be together and partly in search of adventure with tourists passing through, the young and the not so young. There were aristocratic visitors, too, from all over Europe, people of substantial means; one must remember that in those days, not everyone could afford to travel.

In addition to the Europa there was the Grand Hotel, the Danieli, and the Bauer Grünwald, all frequented by these customers, and I started to think: "Why not open a bar, just like the hotel bars but in a *fondamenta* in Venice, an elegant bar, but one customers can enter without running into a gauntlet of porters in braided uniforms or passing through a splendid but intimidating reception hall?"

What I did not have was the money.

I had spent the winter season of 1927 tending bar at the Bellevue Hotel in San Remo, where to my misfortune one of my customers was a certain Mr. Utesky. He was a charming man, self-assured, a good customer, the picture of health, well dressed, suntanned — in short, the classic example of a man who inspires trust. But that type may also be the classic example of the swindler. Isn't a swindler always well mannered and courteous? He spends days or even months working his victims so capably that when he makes his move, it always happens in a way that seems utterly natural, almost what you should have expected all along.

Of course I have met quite a few in my career, bigtime and small-time swindlers, and I must confess that I have even admired some of them for their bravura. There are all types, from the one I have never seen before who rushes in to ask, "Cipriani, I forgot my wallet, could you lend me a thousand lire," to the captain of industry who cheats on the number of sandwiches he has taken from the counter. There are thousands of customers every year who take an ashtray to add to their collection, all of them respectable people, people who have never stolen a thing in their life.

One evening a customer leaned over to me and whispered, "Look at the lady. She just put a table napkin in her purse."

"Are you sure?" I asked.

"Positive."

A difficult and rather embarrassing situation, but after a moment's thought I realized how to deal with it: I added an item to the tab, "export: 2,500 lire."

The woman asked for the bill, looked at it, and called the waiter. Then the waiter called me.

"What's this export?" she asked.

"That's the napkin, madame. But if you prefer, we could exchange it for an ashtray, which is cheaper."

"Fine," she said without batting an eye. She took the napkin out of her purse, and I brought her an ashtray, neatly wrapped up in plain brown paper.

But I was talking about Mr. Utesky, a great gambler at the casino and endowed with all the qualities I mentioned. I still remember his incredible skill in getting me to lend him all my earnings for the season. He disappeared at once, and I never saw him again. I was disheartened when I returned to Venice, not least because it was no easy matter to explain to Giulietta what had happened.

I went back to the Europa for the summer season, on my guard against swindlers, of course, but the experience with Mr. Utesky had not diminished my youthful, trusting nature. And it was a good thing, because if I had been any less open to new acquaintances, I would not have gotten to know the young man without whom Harry's Bar would never have progressed beyond the status of a mere pipe dream.

Harry Pickering, a quiet young student, was American. He was staying in the hotel with an old aunt, the aunt's young companion, and a dog. All of them were regular customers of the Europa bar.

Harry's family had sent him off to Italy with his aunt to treat an early form of alcoholism. But he was bored traveling the world without friends of his own, and he was drowning his boredom in cocktails. The aunt and her young friend were always good-humored, and the Pekingese was resigned. The little entourage did not see much of Venice, perhaps a glimpse of Piazza San Marco once a day, but they saw a lot of the bar. With light and easy smiles they ordered every kind of liquor, preferably strong cocktails, but their old faithful was always a

double bourbon and 7UP, something fizzy to remind them that their throats were still there.

They started about eleven in the morning. They
would sit at the bar for aperitifs, have lunch on the terrace overlooking the Grand Canal, and come back to the
bar for a drink in the afternoon. The evening was the
same. Anyone who wanted to open a small bar would
have made a fair profit serving just the three of them,
especially Harry, the least cheerful of the group.

They had been at the Europa for two months
when Harry had an argument with his aunt and her
gigolo, who checked out and left him alone with the dog.
This did not keep Harry from the bar, but he drank less
and less. I was alarmed by this unforeseen change in his
habits, and I tried to discover the reason for it. I surmised
that either Mr. Pickering was ill, or his money was running out. The latter idea was the right one. After a few
days, I asked if he needed money. He looked surprised,
but hopeful as well.

"Why," he asked, "would you lend me money?"

"If you need it," I replied.

So, trying to drive visions of Utesky out of my
mind and finding the courage to tell Giulietta, I decided
to lend him ten thousand lire, a lot of money for a simple
bartender like myself who had started out earning three
lire an hour in a pastry shop.

He went off happy, and rather less happy than
he, I was left to wait. A month went by, then another,
and not a word. But I was sure I had not made a mistake. This Mr. Pickering had to be a decent boy. It was

written all over his face. That was the winter of 1930. America was in the throes of the Great Depression, but I never lost hope. Finally on a cold February morning I saw him come into the bar. He made quite a fuss over me.

"Cipriani, thank you so much. Here is your money. And to show you how grateful I am, take this as well. We can use it to open a bar together."

"This as well" was forty thousand lire.

"Let's call it Harry's Bar," he said.

And I was happy.

One morning a few days later, someone knocked on the glass window that opened onto the *calle* behind the Europa bar. It was Giulietta. "Giuseppe," she said, "I've found Harry's Bar."

Fifteen feet by thirty, it was the cordage warehouse, and it was up for rent. There was even room for a small kitchen and a storage room in the back.

I liked it at once because it was at the end of a dead-end street. At that time there was no bridge connecting the street to Piazza San Marco. This meant that the customers would have to come there on purpose, and couldn't just stop in as they were passing by. That is the way I wanted it. To this day people have to come to Harry's Bar on purpose. And as if to emphasize this fact, we have no sign, only the name etched in the windowpanes.

At that time the Baron Gianni Rubin de Cervin,

who owned the beautiful Palazzo Albrizzi and later became the director of the Naval Museum in Venice, was among the young customers of the bar at the Europa. I asked him to help me decorate the bar.

He understood the effect I wanted, and he had a real gift for seeing how to achieve it. In the years I worked in hotels I had learned what should be done and, more important, what should be avoided. I wanted a simple, elegant place with two essential features: the customers must not feel oppressed by the decor, and there had to be light. I never liked dark places; darkness serves to hide something, and people only whisper in the dark.

The interior Cervin designed was pure art deco with hand-painted marine motifs and figures on the walls; it looked more like a ship's bar than one on land. Near the actual bar he placed large armchairs, which were soon replaced with smaller armchairs, where people could sit and eat the few dishes — often cooked by my wife — that were served in those early years.

Baron Gianni lived well into his eighties, and to the end of his life he came to Harry's Bar every day for a drink or two and would usually end up staying for a meal. I had originally offered him a partnership in Harry's Bar in return for doing the decor, but he had refused, preferring to be paid in cash. For the rest of his life he complained that he had made a terrible mistake in not taking me up on my first offer.

I myself designed special three-legged tables that would not tip or wobble on the uneven floor. The bar itself, which stretched right up to the door, offered an immediately accessible support for the shy and insecure. I'll never cease to be amazed at how shy people can be; perhaps everyone is slightly shy, even the ones who seem least so.

There were some compulsory requirements in Harry's Bar. The space was what it was, so the tables, for example, while they had to be comfortable, had to be small as well. And everything else had to be in proportion, including plates, glassware, and silver. Luxury restaurants — it was certainly the case then and to some extent even today — crushed the diner under a mountain of heavy silver that only a giant could handle with any ease. So I miniaturized, which is to say that, for Harry's Bar, I decided on dessert knives, forks, and spoons, which are elegant, light, and well balanced. I didn't want my customers to have to be weight lifters to enjoy a meal.

A hundred little things go into making a success in my business. For example, I have always considered it a question of honor to make sure that someone dining on shrimps does not get a whiff of codfish cooking on the stove. Where smell is concerned, the kitchen has nothing to do with the dining room.

I went into business on May 13, 1931.

If all the people who claimed to have been the first to set foot in Harry's Bar had actually come the first day of business, the bar would have had to be as big as Piazza San Marco. It was an immediate success. One of my colleagues from the old days at the Hôtel Monaco joined me, a waiter named Toffolo who was mad about cooking.

Berto Toffolo — he now has his own restaurant in the Friuli region, about fifty miles outside of Venice — was a small wonder in the kitchen. I will never forget his shrimp risotto, the crayfish Armorican; and most of all his hot and cold sandwiches. He was an incredible man. The bar could be full of diners, but everything around him was always in perfect order as he worked in the kitchen. It all looked as if he had nothing to do, yet nobody was kept waiting a minute longer than necessary.

One of my first customers was an extremely serious, formal Englishman who drank much and spoke little, partly because he had an incredible stammer. To have any kind of extended conversation with him meant abandoning the other diners and dedicating half a day to him. He stayed at a nearby hotel and would take the few steps to the bar, climb onto a stool, and daintily sip three or four martinis. His fairly pale forehead would color slightly as the alcohol got the blood moving, loosening his tongue enough to order a fifth martini with hardly a stutter or stammer.

I had no idea what his business was, nor did I care to. All I knew was his name, Colin Hawks, because once, when he was less tongue-tied than usual, he managed to utter it in one breath. Sometimes he took his glass to a table, brought tiny scraps of paper out of his pocket, and covered them with a minute dense script.

One day Mr. Hawks came into Harry's Bar carrying a suitcase. "I'm l-leaving," he stammered. I offered him my hand across the bar; he took it and held it while he uttered what must have been the longest speech he had held in months. Between stammers of every kind, he asked me how to get to the garage in Piazzale Roma on foot. He wanted to walk. He had become so enamored of my bar that he had spent most of his days and evenings there and had seen very little of Venice.

What could I say? Go outside, walk straight ahead, turn right, then left, and then ask once, twice, ten times what direction to go? With his speech difficulty, it would have taken him a week at least.

"Mr. Hawks," I said reassuringly, "if you can wait half an hour till I'm free, I will walk you there."

Thirty minutes went by, I took off my white jacket, and off we went. We ambled slowly through *campi* and *campielli*, past *corti* and *fondamente*. I played guide, and he just beamed. Some of his pleasure may have come from not having to express his admiration for the city in speech. When we reached the garage, he put his suitcase in the trunk, shook my hand and thanked me, and then drove off.

A couple of weeks later, a customer burst into the bar waving a copy of the *London Daily Mail*.

"Cipriani, this is about you!"

Me, in the newspaper? I was excited, and frightened too. I quickly examined my conscience: Had I unintentionally offended some peer in incognito who was getting me back by telling the world of his misadventures in Venice? Not at all. The newspaper addressed its readers, loyal subjects of the crown, more or less in this vein:

> If you happen to be in Venice and want to know something about the city, forget the travel agencies and the tourist offices. Go to Harry's Bar. There you will find Giuseppe Cipriani, who can satisfy your every need. Go see him, and you will suddenly find yourself in a friendly city welcoming you with open arms.

I looked at the byline. Colin Hawks worked for the *Daily Mail*. And what a splendid way he had chosen to thank me for a simple courtesy!

A great many articles have been published about Harry's Bar since then. Thousands of things have been written in pursuit of the secret of its success. Dozens upon dozens of journalists have given their own versions of what Harry's Bar is to them. I think the real secret, however, is that there is no secret. Anyone who visits Harry's Bar always finds three things: quality, a smile, and simplicity.

It is not true, for example, that the secret of a good barman is the strange concoctions he invents. If you discount the short-lived aberrations that unscrupulous bartenders occasionally invent in an effort to stir up a little profitable notoriety at the expense of their customers' stomachs, there are actually very few variations on the five possible starting points of any cocktail: gin, vodka, whiskey, cognac, and rum. The classic drinks can be counted on the fingers of one hand. The trick is to make them well — conscientiously, and, as in everything, with love — and to fit them to the particular taste of the individual drinker, and even to his various moods. In fact, a good barman will never make the drinks exactly the same. With one glance, he has to sense whether his customer wants to have his martini drier than usual, or sweeter. And he should have the drinks waiting for his regulars before they appear at the door.

In the course of my career as a barman I have had my share of strange requests. Take the martini, for example. Hemingway smiled when he ordered a "Montgomery," which he explained was a martini made with the same proportion of gin to vermouth that the famous British general preferred when he led his soldiers against the enemy — fifteen to one.

One customer liked me to pour a little vermouth over the ice in the shaker and then throw it out before adding the gin. He called it an in-and-out martini. Another one asked me to show the vermouth bottle to the gin bottle but not to put any in his martini.

These special tastes aside, a good martini has to be dry, icy, undiluted, and served in the right amount in the right glass. The bona fide martini drinker sips it very slowly, drop by drop.

One summer day a party of six Italians came in and ordered six martinis. They may have been expecting a sweet vermouth martini, but in any case they liked what they got — ice cold, dry, and strong. They poured it down in a single gulp and then went out.

They came back half an hour later, all in good spirits, and ordered six more martinis. The men in the group had pinned little notes on their lapels. That piqued my curiosity, and I leaned forward to see what was written: "We have to return to Mantua. Whoever finds us, please get us to the garage in Piazzale Roma by six thirty A.M."

I have always avoided making a show of preparing a cocktail. There are bartenders who look like marionettes the way they move, the way they handle the shaker, flipping bottles into the air and catching them in flight. I wouldn't be surprised if they used canned orange juice!

People who have something they want to forget usually order a martini — maybe because it is strong and dry. I have never seen anyone drown his sorrows in champagne.

I remember an old customer, a German prince who had married an extremely wealthy woman and who for a long time came to Harry's Bar every evening for a single martini. One evening he came in as usual, drank his martini, and immediately ordered a second one. I gave him another, and then another again. Gradually, his face began to sag more and more.

"Something wrong?" I asked.

"A lot," he said, "almost everything. My wife has decided she is going to sleep with her lover tonight in my house!"

I was familiar with his situation, and knew full well that his wife's millions gave his domestic tragedy an almost comic flavor. I also knew he had a keen sense of humor. So I leaned over the counter, and lowering my voice, I asked, "Tell me something, do you want to get a job?"

"I don't know," he replied. "I've never had one."

"Do you have enough to live on?"

He gave me a sad look and shook his head.

"In that case," I said, "I know you have a beautiful house in the country. I'll fix you another martini, then you call a taxi. Go to the country, sleep on it overnight, and then forget about it. Tomorrow is another day, and things will look different. Think of it as a necessity."

"Do you think that's a good idea?"

"I think it's the best idea."

He came back the next day. He had his old aplomb and seemed to be in excellent humor.

"Sleep well?" I asked.

"Like a baby. Thanks for your advice, Cipriani."

And Harry?

From the very beginning, Harry Pickering loved Harry's Bar almost more than I did, so much so, in fact, that in the early years he was without a doubt his own best customer. He took his habitual seat at the bar, drank to his heart's content, and then went back to his hotel, happy as an onion in a Gibson. But the day-to-day responsibilities of running the business were not for him.

When he broached the idea of selling me his share a few years later, I cast about for a way to find the necessary money. Before long, I had managed to save up a sum that was almost equal to the tab he had run up at the bar, and when we added it all together, it was more than what we'd agreed on. After that, he drank a little less, but whenever he was in Venice, he was still one of our best customers.

Here ends the autobiography of Giuseppe Cipriani, and here begins the story told by Arrigo Cipriani.

3

BELLINIS IN PARADISE

I STILL FIND IT HARD TO BELIEVE that my father is dead and gone forever.

After a violent influenza, he insisted on being released from the hospital and going back home. There was a childlike cunning in the way he convinced the doctors that in his own room, he would have everything he needed, from a call bell to his eyeglasses, ten pairs of them. He was always fumblingly putting them on and taking them off, and each time he would look around with the curiosity of a blind man seeing things for the first time. In fact, he already knew the end was at hand. He was so in touch with his brain that he could even show me where the seat of his illness was. "Something happened here," he would say, pointing to a spot behind one of those big ears of his. "This is where the trouble is, but they," indicating the whole hospital, "don't believe me."

He hadn't been back home long before he had the first real signs that his absentmindedness was taking on a new dimension. He could never find things when he looked for them. I scotch-taped the bell to the head of the bed and put his glasses in the special place he indicated to his left. We all did everything we could for him. But life seemed to trickle drop by drop into his nearly invisible veins, only to rush out again with piercing pain.

All the while, he held on to his sense of humor. The house was filled with glucose drips, and he would wink at me: "Arrigo, things couldn't be better." He pronounced the whole disease a farce and managed more than once to convince us all. When the long sleeping began, he would wake up incredibly refreshed and come out with marvelous remarks, flashes of love, and uncomplaining sweetness. Once, after sleeping for three or four days straight, he woke up and, seeing the whole family gathered around his bed, looked me in the eye. With perfectly feigned seriousness he asked, "Are we all dead?"

At Easter he told me to bring him some champagne. I moistened his lips with it, and he blew me a kiss. "Get drunk on the rest," he said in a feeble voice.

Three weeks later, he started taking strange and increasingly deep and infrequent breaths, and life went out of him. It was a Saturday evening, and I am sure he planned it that way. "Sunday they work," he must have thought, "and Monday they have nothing to do, because the bar is closed, so they can have the funeral then."

All I remember of his dead body is the very pale, calm drawn face and the suit hanging on his legs the way only dead men's suits do. The undertaker turned up his nose at the idea of the pine coffin my father wanted, but we finally found one in Mestre. A few years before, when I commented on an expensive cashmere jacket he had bought for himself, my father had responded without blinking an eye: "It didn't cost me a thing. I just decided that I want a simple pine coffin when I die instead of the fancy stuff. The money you're going to save — that's what paid for the jacket."

The coffin looked homemade. We found some blunt screwdrivers to fasten the lid. It sat slightly askew on our shoulders, because my son Giuseppe is six feet tall, I'm five eight, I don't remember who the other man was, and then there was Sandrino, who had worked at Harry's Bar for more years than anyone could remember. Everyone called him the ebullient mouse man because he was just "five lire" tall.

There were seven splendid gondolas. "Make sure all the brass is polished," my father had instructed me, and it was. The weather was cold, and a sharp wind drove low gray clouds before us. When we came abreast of Harry's Bar the storm burst, just the way he liked it. Then we reached the Rio della Paglia, a turn to the right and then left as far as the hospital, and finally out into the wind with all the motorboats and *vaporini* slowing down to watch those seven gondolas and their sixteen magnificent gondoliers.

There was something cheerful and weddinglike

in the air. We reminded one another of the acute observations my father used to make, of his simplicity, and of the humorous way he dealt with things that would make anyone else weep. We carried him on our shoulders inside the cemetery, the most beautiful cemetery in the world, in my opinion. A moment to look at the coffin on the ground before the rapid shoveling covered it in a matter of moments. He was buried according to his wishes, between two strangers, with the openness of a man who seeks out others to share life with and also to share death with.

I imagine that one day I, too, will get up there, and a nice solemn voice will say: "Besides all the other bad things you have done, now this!"

And I will ask, "What?" pretending not to understand.

"You know perfectly well what. You did not have a blessing said for your father at his grave."

"But he didn't want a blessing to be said." He had never had anything to do with the church and refused to talk to a priest, even on his deathbed.

"How do you know? He might have changed his mind at the last moment, for example."

"Pardon me, but would a blessing have made any difference?"

"You are ignorant, impertinent, and also a sinner."

"In that case I apologize. I only asked because a moment ago I thought I had a glimpse of him over there, with that bearded writer. And don't tell me they were not drinking a bellini together. But forgive me."

That is how I think I will catch up with him, probably by the skin of my teeth. He showed me so many things, but I'm sure he had a great many other things he wanted to show me as well, not to mention all the things he will have thought of since his arrival there.

In the meantime, he will surely have persuaded them to change the color of the sky, make the stars shine brighter, and shift some inconvenient cloud, because I know that is what he is like, the way we all knew him.

4

HARD ACT TO FOLLOW

I FINISHED THE CLASSIC LYCEUM at the age of eighteen, and after a couple of weeks of vacation and a major discussion, most of it a one-way discussion, about the university department I should enroll in, the family, which is to say my father, decided I should study law.

Just upstairs from Harry's Bar was the office of Ferruccio Ferrarin, a criminal lawyer of the old school, and Ferrarin had been our customer since the day the bar opened. So after a brief negotiation between Mr. Ferrarin and my father, the terms of which I was never told, I was shut up in a windowless little room to work as his clerk.

I knew absolutely nothing about law, one reason being that since the end of World War I — after the glut of murders and killings in which the dead were the guilty and the murderers the heroes — there had been little talk about law in Italy. But I thoroughly enjoyed accompanying the lawyer to the courthouses in all the little towns in the Veneto, not only because of the excitement of the court trials, but because he had an absolutely terrifying way of driving his sports car. He had a tic: he would shut both eyes for three or four endless seconds and twist his face in a variety of grimaces, preferably when he was doing close to a hundred miles an hour with an enormous trailer truck coming in the opposite direction. I sat by his side ready to grab the wheel a second before we crashed.

The trials themselves were fun to watch too, but I noticed that Ferrarin's speeches made more of an impression on me and the loafers and idlers who always attend criminal trials than on the judges, who tended to nod off, only to be awakened brusquely by the lawyer's thundering voice. On the whole he won very few cases, but his clients always seemed extremely gratified by his high-sounding discourses. They may not have been much use, but they were totally fascinating, especially if you didn't understand what he was saying, and most of all because they made the accused feel certain he was getting his money's worth.

Then the day came for my first examination. My father greeted me early in the morning before he left the house, and my mother was rather emotional as she saw me off, as if I were leaving for the Crusades. I took that first examination about two in the afternoon and barely passed. I called home at three o'clock to give the news and was ordered to report to the cash register at Harry's Bar at 6:00 on the dot.

"You'll never be a great lawyer," my father said with absolute conviction. "So you'd better get used to working here."

My father's remark is still vivid in memory. At the time I never even thought of challenging it. It is probably just as well that things turned out as they did. Later in life I found that what may at first seem like a defeat or a sacrifice subsequently proves to be an absolute necessity and the source of future benefits. Lino Toffolo, a great Venetian comic actor, once told me that when he was a boy his father often said: "Since you're an idiot, you'll make a good infantryman." You might think that his father's drastic judgment would have created tragic mental problems for the boy Lino, but it did not. Toffolo became one of the finest comic actors in the Venetian dialect.

My father was concerned by the near failure of my first exam, but he never even considered the idea of taking me out of school. The cash register was simply my first taste of a job — a safety valve, a warning that work represented the real world. But he expected me to keep up my studies all the while.

So I kept my nose to the grindstone, and somehow I managed to pass all five of my examinations that first year and the next year as well. At the same time, I worked at Harry's Bar a couple of days a week and almost every evening after ten o'clock, when my father went home. The cash register was a very old American NCR, which had taken the place of an Italian RIV that was always breaking down. RIV was a well-known Italian ball-bearing company. My father had a remarkable sense of humor, and he suggested that the Germans lost the war because they used RIV ball bearings in the wheels of their tanks.

I cannot honestly say that I paid much attention to my surroundings in those first years of work at Harry's Bar. I don't think I really understood all that much about how things were done there. I'm not sure I did even when my father retired, and at the tender age of twenty-five I took over the family business.

The Zen masters preach that their disciples should kill the Buddha, their friends and relatives, and their own fathers. Stuff and nonsense, if you ask me. I have never understood this business about inborn patricidal wishes, though I admit I have occasionally noticed in my own children a faint tendency to wish me dead. They accuse me of being authoritarian and making everyone else's decisions, and they tell me that, in this regard as in all others, I'm the opposite of my own father. But this just goes to show that they knew Giuseppe Cipriani only in his old age, when he always played the part of the overindulgent grandfather. When I compare myself with him, my impression is that I am far too permissive and accommodating.

Kill my father? The thought never even crossed my mind. I never ceased to be fascinated by him — by my father, the man the Zen masters would have advised me to kill so that I could continue to live. I remember the simplicity of his every gesture, the delicacy of his hands as he shook a tower of ice, and the light touch he applied to everything he did.

That was probably when I understood, albeit unconsciously, the importance of adjectives in our lives, the meaning that they give to the work of man. There are myriad ways of doing things, and each of them can be described with extraordinary precision. How? With adjectives. We had a very snobbish customer, and whenever you asked how the food was, he would always reply, "Divine." It was the only adjective he knew. He may have been exaggerating a bit, but I think he meant to say that everyone involved in preparing that dish and in serving it had worked in the rarefied air that surrounds the gods.

From the very first days I was put in charge of Harry's Bar, I was constantly struck by how different I was from my father. For one thing, I have never been able to take things in at a glance the way he could. He seemed to see things from four different directions all at once, north, south, east, and west. I on the other hand was totally caught up lazily absorbing reality the way a sponge absorbs the water it is dropped in. But one thing I can say: I was never sorry to be working in Harry's Bar. I cannot say that it was fun, but I was never bored.

I managed to survive relatively intact the first weeks on my own. The only thing that sometimes upset my psychophysical balance was the remark of longtime customers when they entered:

"Where's Cipriani?"

I would timidly raise my hand, and they would continue: "No, not you. I mean *Cipriani*," referring, of course, to my father. Someone else in my place might have tried to reserve a seat on a psychoanalyst's couch to recount the first time he had been told how babies were born. But in my case, these bored refusals to acknowledge me as a human being left me indifferent. Indeed, these were precisely the remarks that stimulated me. I immediately wanted to win these people over. Perhaps helped by my youth — which is forgiven everything — and a bit by the good disposition of the customers as well, I often succeeded.

I remember one winter evening in particular. There were few people in the bar. I called home near midnight. I always called to give my father a progress report: to tell him how things were going, how many customers had come in after he left, and how sales had been.

"How's business?" he asked. These nightly conversations always began the same way.

"Not too bad."

"How many meals did you serve?"

"Twenty-one."

"Who did you have?"

"No one special. Except maybe Camillo della Noce."

"Say hello to him, but be careful! Don't even think of lending him any money."

As I was soon to learn for myself, Harry's Bar was

full of people like Count Camillo della Noce. From the very beginning, a lot of my father's customers were aristocrats, but in an age when aristocrats didn't necessarily have a lot of money — often because they'd spent it all in hotels and restaurants, which is why they were so important for the restaurant business. Count della Noce was just such a nobleman. He was from an old Friuli family, he had a beautiful house in the country, rented a small apartment in Venice, and he knew just about everybody. Later he became good friends with Ernest Hemingway and with all of Hemingway's friends as well. And like all good aristocrats, he had never worked a day in his life. Small wonder he was always broke. But he was a very charming man.

When I went to his table to give him my father's regards, he immediately classified me among the people whose only concern was to make his life pleasurable. He thanked me for my father's greeting and said: "By the way, Arrigo, would you bring me two hundred thousand lire in cash. I'll give you a check later." I did not have the nerve to object, partly because I thought that, after all, it was a matter of cashing a check, not making a loan.

About one in the morning, when all the other customers had gone home, the count stood up and came to the cash register.

"Do you have my money?"

"Yes, sir." I handed him the money and waited for his check.

The count put the money in his pocket. He put

his other hand in his other pocket and said: "Arrigo, I forgot my checkbook. I'll pay you tomorrow."

He was out the door at once, and I was dumbfounded.

That was almost forty years ago, when 200,000 lire were worth at least $1,000.

The only choice open to me at that moment was escape to America. What could I possibly say to my father, especially after what he had told me?

So, after ten minutes of terrible consternation and feverish brain racking, I decided to spend the night in pursuit of Count della Noce and the money. I looked for him at the Martini dance hall. No luck. I tried a couple of other places that kept late hours. Still no count. Finally fortune smiled. At about three o'clock in the morning, I found him at the Ciro Bar.

I asked the barman to call him. He greeted me with a noisy enthusiasm that palled as soon as I told him why I had come: I had given him the money from my own pocket, and the next morning I would have to answer for it to my father. So would he be so kind as to return the money at once?

The count fully understood my situation and my state of mind. He even tried to console me. "But, Arrigo," he said, "I still have to make a call at the casino. Rest assured that tomorrow morning I'll bring you your money." He gave me a hearty pat on the back, and I found myself outside the bar, more disheartened and terrified than before.

But at that hour of night there was nothing left to

do but go home. I tiptoed up to my room for fear of wak-ing my father, who, I was sure, would immediately ask how things had gone with Count della Noce.

About five in the morning, as I tossed terrified in my bed, I decided to make another attempt. I knew that the count lived at the Hotel Luna, which is almost next door to Harry's Bar, so I called the hotel. I pretended that I had an urgent need to speak with him, and the switchboard operator connected me with the room. A deep sleepy voice answered and asked who in the world was the pest who dared wake him at dawn, a time of the day the count was familiar with only from descriptions in books. I told him who I was, and he asked what in the world I wanted.

"Well, Count, it is about that money," I replied. "You see, I really need to get it back."

He did not seem to welcome my request. He blurted out something and then slammed down the receiver.

Still, I was encouraged by the partial success of actually reaching him by phone, so I tried again with the same story at six o'clock, and then again at seven, when I crept out of the house to avoid an encounter with my father.

By eight o'clock I was at Harry's Bar supervising the cleaning. We usually open our doors about ten thirty. At nine o'clock the count appeared at the service en-trance. As soon as he saw me, he pulled out a sheaf of banknotes and slammed them on the counter.

"Never again," he thundered, "never again will I

ask you for a loan. And now, if you please," he added in a somewhat milder tone, "let me have a cup of coffee, and don't expect me to pay for it, for heaven's sake."

He was a man of the world, a good man, intelligent and charming. He lived with his aged mother, who kept a very tight hold on the purse strings. And perhaps she knew what she was doing. When she finally died, he was not slow to follow her, burned out by the constant revelry he had spent his inheritance on.

He had a soft spot for me. But after that episode he never even thought of asking me for a cent; on the contrary, he was scrupulous about paying his checks. The only tab he left unpaid was his last one, for the simple reason that he had spent his entire inheritance. I was very sad to hear of his death, not because of his unpaid tab, of course, but because a representative of an important era had gone. He was one of the last real patricians that I was lucky enough to have known. A true gentleman, albeit with little money.

Count della Noce was not the only favored customer of Harry's Bar whose pocketbook was leaner than his appetite. I remember that my old high-school teacher, Professor Alexander Vardaniga, found himself in a similar position toward the end of his life. He had made a terrible mistake when he retired by donating his enormous collection of books to the Church and was promised a modest pension in return. The Church kept the books but refused to pay him his pension, saying his library was not as valuable as he had claimed. After that, Professor Vardaniga couldn't afford to eat at Harry's Bar anymore, but he still came in for a light snack, and we always served him a full meal even when all he could pay for was the coffee. He had been such a good customer for so many years, how could we let him down?

Today, such stories are the stuff of memory. Money is money, and there's no room for ambiguity in financial affairs. But we did not do business that way at Harry's Bar. For my father, money was important to keep the business alive, and for no other reason than that. If I ever went to the trouble to add up all the tabs that were never paid at Harry's Bar, it would probably go into the millions.

Fortunately, I've never gone to the trouble.

5

FASCISM, WAR, AND THE BAR ARRIGO

My FATHER DIDN'T SHARE MUCH with me about events, customers, and the ways of the world in the years before World War II. For one thing, I didn't see much of him, for the simple reason that when you have a restaurant, you're never home at mealtimes. It was late in the evening when he came home, so I wondered then — and now I know — how my father and mother found time to talk, to share things, and to make love the way other mortals do, those who are not in the restaurant business. I mention this for the benefit of those who, unaware of the drawbacks, think that owning a restaurant must be fascinating and who also harbor a secret unsatisfied wish to have a restaurant of their own. When someone doesn't know what to do with a country villa that he's inherited and asks me for advice about opening a small hotel and dining room, I always reply, "Don't do it!" Not unless you have a great passion, total dedication, and a longing to serve, to suffer, and to love that goes far beyond the daydreams of an amateur with an elegant old drawing room.

In any case, what Italy had in the years leading up to World War II was primarily fascism, at least that is how it looked to us. And the fear that poisoned my childhood has always made me hate fascism. I will never forget the terror of the war, the loss of freedom, the fear of talking in a normal voice because you could never be sure who might be listening. I remember trembling as I listened to the forbidden broadcasts of Radio London, but also feeling heroic, as if for a moment I were part of a plot to overthrow some great, idiotic monster. In those days we believed that the monster would die once and for all. Now I know that it's not enough to slay fascism, but that we would need to stomp out everything that ends in *-ism* — all those blind irrational credos that transport human beings to the lowest depths of inhumanity.

The fascist owners of the leading hotel chains in those troubled years could not understand the success of Harry's Bar, especially since it had an English name and was deemed somehow different from the Italic race. They never missed a chance to harass my father. For years, they spread the rumor that Harry's Bar was a den of homosexuals — a very serious issue for fascist males.

And then there was talk that it was the meeting place of Jews and antifascists. Every now and then groups of fascist party members would come to dinner and, on the pretext that the service was bad, they would lay the place to waste. This was usually during the winter, when the summer clientele, the tourists and the aristocrats, was not around to witness the destruction.

At that time the cook in the tiny kitchen was a former coworker of my father from his early days. He had cooked for the staff at the Hôtel Monaco, which meant he had started the hard way. The staff members were really difficult customers — more difficult than the most demanding diners. It is always like that. It is much harder to satisfy people who are accustomed to bad eating at home than people who are accustomed to good food and understand it.

This modest cook, Berto Toffolo, did everything on the four burners of the stove, following recipes that he developed with my father. That was when Casanova sole was invented, when crayfish Armorican was modified, as well as the *croque monsieur* and the cream crepes. We still serve these dishes, and they are as good as they ever were. I believe there is a sort of universal taste that is common to all peoples, regardless of what tastes they favor in their own country. I have always found that the food we serve at Harry's Bar appeals equally to customers from every country, and that our regulars never tire of eating what we cook. Not all cuisines have this universal appeal: even when I dine at a fine Chinese or Spanish restaurant, I seldom want to return the very next evening.

But we have always had customers of every nationality come back to Harry's Bar night after night to savor the dishes Berto Toffolo and my father invented together in the difficult decade after 1930.

Then the war came.

The first tangible effect of World War II on Harry's Bar was that we were required to change its "odious" English name: instead of Harry's Bar, it became Bar Arrigo. My father was also forced to put up a sign: JEWS NOT WELCOME. Federico Kechler, a steady patron and a man of extreme sensitivity, came in one morning shortly afterward and removed the sign to the kitchen, where it remained until the new cook, Enrico Caniglia, took it down some time later.

Enrico Caniglia came from the Abruzzi region, and he was as capable as he was modest and grumpy. He worked at Harry's Bar until the 1980s and never once set foot in the dining room. If you told him a joke, he laughed at it two days later. He worked seventy hours a week and was persuaded to change his trousers only after we started cutting an inch off the bottoms every day. He and my father had a real partnership. Together they decided what to add to the menu, and all the typical Harry's Bar dishes were born during the thirties and early forties. Before we had written menus, my father told people what they could eat, and he gave no prices. Then we started having a written menu but still without prices. The prices were made to order.

Years later, when the time came for Caniglia to retire, I told him, "Enrico, I think that if you stop working all at once, you might die." He had worked too hard all his life to just stop and do nothing day after day. So we agreed that he would work four or five years more, but each year one day less per week. And so it was. There were customers so fond of him that before he retired once and for all, they would come to eat only on the days he was in the kitchen. The countess Natalia Volpi, God rest her soul, claimed that the risotto with peas was never good on the days Caniglia wasn't there. It was not true, but I'm sure it seemed true to her, which is all that matters.

The most important employee at Harry's Bar during the war years was a Swiss, Renato Hausamann. My father had hired him in 1934, when Renato and some fifty other hopefuls, economic victims of the Great Depression, answered an ad in the paper for a junior waiter. Renato was the only applicant who admitted he had never worked in a bar before. He was a young boy at the time, barely fourteen, with a quick and clever air about him. He became a great barman, and was soon the only man my father trusted enough to let him run Harry's Bar in his absence. Shortly before the war broke out, Renato told my father he wanted to become an Italian citizen. My father advised him against this step, and that saved his life. Every week throughout the war, he received a package full of all kinds of good things from the International Red Cross.

Then came 1943, the year Italy surrendered and Mussolini was deposed. It was a moment of shame to some, but to my mind it has always stood out as one of the more illustrious moments in Italian history. Mussolini was ousted on July 25. As of July 24, Italy had approximately forty-nine million fascists, and the very next day there was not a single fascist to be found anywhere in the country. There was not even the trace of a fascist. I say this with some pride, because it means that in Italy, good sense counts for more than blind faith.

In any case, on September 8, 1943, King Victor Emmanuel III and his faithful marshal General Badoglio signed an armistice with the Allies. And barely half an hour later they did something that demonstrated great courage — they sailed for Egypt and left Italy and its army to deal on their own with the wrath of their former German allies. Almost overnight, the Germans occupied all of Northern Italy, and they lost no time freeing Mussolini, who promptly founded the Republic of Salò, so called because his government set up its headquarters in that delightful town on Lake Garda. He could no longer rule from Rome, since that city had been liberated by the Allies.

During this terrible period from 1943 to 1945, when Venice was occupied by the Germans while the south of Italy could breathe free, Harry's Bar — pardon me, the Bar Arrigo — was requisitioned by the fascists and turned into a mess hall for Mussolini's navy. Someone had taken his revenge.

So my father left his trusted Renato Hausamann in charge of the bar and stayed home. He had given

shelter to the whole family of his brother, my uncle
Enrico, who was in the stocking business in Verona and
had moved to Venice because it had not been bombed.
My father made fresh bread and sweets every day, and
my aunt Adelia, Enrico's wife, rolled out *tagliatelle* so
fine and delicious that they could make you lose your
mind. My mother cooked the main dishes, and my aunt
Gabriella, heedless of the bombing and machine-gun
fire, went to the countryside once a week to buy black
market chickens from the peasants, as well as eggs, flour,
and whatever else she could find to feed us. Between fathers, mothers, children, and grandchildren, there were
twelve of us, and we all lived in the same small house.

And soon there were at least five or six additional
hungry customers who stopped by in the evenings for
an aperitif and stayed on for dinner. With my father's
less-than-tacit approval, the word had spread among the
habitués of Harry's Bar that while the Germans occupied what they believed was the restaurant of Giuseppe
Cipriani, Mr. Cipriani would be happy to serve his former
customers a fine meal and a glass of wine at his private
residence.

So our fears during these trying times were, if
not quieted, at least garnished by these crowded, noisy,
and cheerful daily gatherings. My recollections of those
two years at home include a cream puff battle between
a famous Venetian lawyer and a pharmacist who, after a
couple of martinis and a few glasses of white wine, had
dared to suggest that pharmaceutical medicine was far

more important than jurisprudence. The circle of clients also included Signorina Miari, who gave me piano lessons in return for meals. She was a spinster lady who would certainly have starved without us. Whether it was for fear that we might all die from one moment to the next, or because food was the only pleasure possible at the time, the truth is that during these years, lunch and dinner at our house were feasts fit for a king.

In the summer of 1944, my father began to take me out boating every day, sometimes rowing and sometimes sailing. I was still just a boy; machine-gun fire terrified me, and in those days the only things planes did not strafe were the gondolas.

One morning the wind all but dropped and we were almost motionless in front of Ca' Giustinian, the German military headquarters about a hundred yards from Harry's Bar. A horrible explosion suddenly rent the air. All the windows in the palace shattered, and thick black smoke poured out over the Grand Canal. The partisans had bombed it, and two Germans were killed.

Instinctively, my father decided not to go back home. And a good thing it was, because that afternoon a squad of fascist militiamen went to the house to arrest him. If they had found him at home, he would have been shot with six other innocent men, who were executed a few days later on the Riva degli Schiavoni by way of reprisal. They were innocent men. The ones who had planted the bomb were in hiding, although everyone knew who they were.

My father was exonerated the following day, thanks to the esteem the German consul had for him — he had always been impressed by my father's fluency in German — and the fascists were ordered to leave him alone.

This experience did nothing to discourage us from our maritime outings. Almost every day we rowed as far as the entrance to the port, because my father was convinced that the Americans would arrive from the sea. He was right. I will never forget the great experience of standing by the water's edge in front of Harry's Bar at three o'clock on the afternoon of April 25, 1945, to watch the arrival of the foamy amphibious vehicles on the calm water of the Grand Canal, across from Dogana Point. They carried the advance guard of New Zealand liberation troops. What a surprising experience it was, to feel for the first time what seemed like an explosion, an almost painful burst of the gigantic, irresistible emotion of freedom.

Freedom. Not to have seen and felt these things is like never having been in love. I know now that my antifascism will never die.

A few weeks after the liberation, my father was summoned by the U.S. commander of the Allied forces. "You are not a good Italian," he told him sternly.

"Why?" my father asked.

"Because you have not reopened Harry's Bar."

For the first time in his life, my father did not feel inclined to quibble with the authorities.

6

A CAST OF STARS

IT WOULD NOT BE AN EXAGGERATION to say that the years right after the war were years of madness. People of every nationality wanted to have fun, to forget, to celebrate peace.

And then there were the troops. English and American officers came to Harry's Bar every night and drank unbelievable amounts of liquor. The light seemed to have gone out of their glazed eyes, as if they were watching a film with thousands of characters and thousands of situations they could never forget. One evening a group of Australian soldiers decided my father would make a fine rugby ball, and they tossed him from one side of the room to the other as if he were light as a feather. They were not bad fellows. They wanted to have a little fun, and my father, despite himself, was part of it.

But besides playing host to army officers of the various victorious nations after the war, Harry's Bar continued to attract a wide and distinguished clientele. It was in these years that Harry's Bar really became what one could call a watering hole to the rich and famous, and many of the celebrities who started coming to us then have contributed as much to the history of Harry's Bar as those of us who worked there.

One of our most faithful regulars in 1949 and 1950 was Ernest Hemingway. Hemingway had served in Italy during World War I, mostly in the Veneto region, and had covered Italy as a journalist in World War II. He burst into Harry's Bar for the first time in the fall of 1949. While he was to receive the Nobel Prize four years later, literary history and the press had already made him legendary. He divided his time between Harry's Bar in Venice and the island of Torcello in the lagoon, where my father owned a small guesthouse.

The *locanda*, as we all called the little inn, had been offered to us for a modest sum in 1936, and my father had bought it and then left it untouched for several years. He had visited Torcello the first time in 1928, when he took some guests from the Hotel Europa on a gondola excursion around the lagoon. The magic balance between the island's natural beauty and the artful delicacy of the two little churches enchanted him. A host of writers and painters has tried to capture the magic of Torcello, but the island has eluded them all. It looks as if it is floating very slowly on the tide that lazily moves the water in the narrow canals between the grassy banks, and it seems to bear silent and solemn witness to the passage of time.

After the war, my father turned the *locanda* into an idyllic spot with six beautiful guest rooms, a mixed flower and vegetable garden, and a lovely dining room overlooking the ninth-century church — a magical setting. Hemingway occupied a small apartment there named for Santa Fosca, and in the bar he had his own table in one corner, the way he had one in the 1930s at the Closerie des Lilas in Paris. And it was at the *locanda* that I saw him for the first time, when I was still a student in 1950. I had spent a couple of months on the island that spring poring over the textbooks for my first exam. One morning, when I was in the garden, I raised my head and saw this man with a thick gray beard leaning on the windowsill. I had been told who this distinguished guest was. He waved at me, and I responded with a polite, timid bow. I had not read any of his books at the time, but Aunt Gabriella, my mother's sister, who ran the hotel with a sweetness all her own, said he was the greatest writer alive. From my own inexperienced and unsophisticated perspective, I was more impressed by the friendly intimacy of his gesture than by the fact that he was an important figure. In any case, I became used to seeing Hemingway frequently, for he became part of the Cipriani landscape for quite a while.

People still ask about him. There is a nice photograph of him and my father, the two of them wearing enormous sombreros. My father is smiling in the picture, but Hemingway, with his gray beard, looks lost in a dream before a flood of empty glasses. My father and Hemingway had apparently emptied those glasses, and I remember that it took my father three days to recover from his hangover.

That was the first time he ever drank with a customer. My father had a very clear idea of which side of the bar was for the customer and which for the saloonkeeper. He had several favorite rules he liked to follow, the most important of which was that everyone should know his own place. He used to say that he had no friends, only customers, which was true, and he made a point of never crossing the delicate boundary of friendship with a customer. Over the years, countless customers hoped he would become a friend and invited my father to address them with a *tu*. He always responded graciously, but he never complied. "Never say *tu* to a customer," he warned me once, "because there will be a day when he comes in with an important client, or a bigshot friend, or a woman he's trying to impress, and then he won't want to be known as the bartender's buddy." And he was right.

But Hemingway had such a strong personality that there was no chance to keep him at bay. He simply knocked down barriers that did not suit him, even though he was quite capable of putting up his own walls if someone was not to his taste. But that was rare. His patience was much greater than average. There was a magnanimity about him that at times almost seemed excessive;

he filled more pages of his checkbooks than he did novels. That is how generous he was.

He was finishing *Across the River and into the Trees* at the time, and at a certain point in that novel two main characters have a conversation while they are sitting at Harry's Bar. The heroine asks the hero if they can talk about something pleasant. He suggests they look around and speak about the people they see, which strikes her as a fine idea. But no spite, he warns, just wit, yours and mine.

And later in the novel, there is this sensitive description:

> There was no one in Harry's except some early morning drinkers that the Colonel did not know, and two men were doing business at the back of the bar.
>
> There were hours at Harry's when it filled with the people that you knew, with the same rushing regularity as the tide coming in at Mont St. Michel. Except, the Colonel thought, the hours of the tides change each day with the moon, and the hours at Harry's are as the Greenwich Meridian, or the standard meter in Paris, or the good opinion the French military hold of themselves.

Because of pages like that, every now and then someone will say, "Hemingway certainly gave the place good publicity." If the person has a sense of humor, I reply, "You've got it the wrong way around; we gave *him* good publicity. It is no accident that he got the Nobel Prize after he wrote about Harry's Bar, not before."

Hemingway had many good friends in Venice. And aside from his friends, of course, there was a goodly number of snobbish, social-climbing artistic types in search of a little reflected glory. Whenever a cameraman appeared, a group of them would rush to stand next to Hemingway for the photograph. As long as they were a little bit amusing, he let them be.

In fact, I am not convinced that he really was an extrovert at heart. He was just afraid of solitude, and he needed the company of others to keep him distracted. But he was generous in return. My father once told me he knew of a hundred occasions when Hemingway helped young artists.

One of the rare times he lost his calm was when he saw Sinclair Lewis walk into Harry's Bar. As we found out later, Hemingway had no fondness for the author of *Babbitt*. Probably the only thing the two men had in common was their passion for liquor. The minute Lewis walked in, Hemingway described in a few choice words his opinion of the man and then turned away. There was a moment of great tension, but nothing happened. Lewis simply ignored the remark and went to a table. He died in Rome a year later.

Between 1949 and 1950 my father decided to keep the *locanda* on Torcello open for Hemingway even in the winter. The *locanda* became Hemingway's home. The writer was still robust and exuberant, and occasionally, if he found someone strong enough, he good-naturedly showed off his old passion for boxing, even stripping to the waist despite the cold weather. And the boxing match, which never had a winner or a loser, was followed by the inevitable drinking match.

All that winter, while Hemingway appeared to spend the day in total freedom, he was in fact implacably rigorous and precise about his work. Every evening at ten, with extremely rare exceptions, he closed up shop and went to his apartment to write. He would order six bottles of a Verona wine, Amarone, which lasted the night. In the morning we would find the empties.

Sometimes he would go out duck hunting in the early morning. The winter of '49 was an extremely cold one, but without the damp fog that sometimes obscures the lagoon. Occasionally he would leave Venice and drive a monumental convertible to Cortina for the skiing. Friends said he would arrive blue in the face with his beard completely frozen.

As it turned out, that winter he spent in Venice was one of the last great seasons of his life. When he came back again in 1954, he was already a bit sad. He told my father that Gordon's gin was the world's best antiseptic. But perhaps even he no longer believed that. His health was failing, and an airplane accident in Africa a few years later was the last straw. When in 1963 he realized that because of his health he could no longer live as he wished, he chose his own way out.

You could hear Orson Welles's laugh halfway up Calle Vallaresso. He was as big as an armoire, and he always had an appetite to match when he walked through the door of Harry's Bar. And an even bigger thirst. He immediately ate two plates of shrimp sandwiches and washed them down with two bottles of iced Dom Perignon. And then he would lean back in his chair and look around with a contented air. He was a lion with the whole world but a puppy with his wife, the Italian actress Paola Mori. I watched him one morning at breakfast, after a night carousing without her at the Martini dance hall. His head was lowered, and he didn't utter a word the whole time she angrily berated him. His grumpiness was only a façade; he was warm and generous. He was disorganized and often forgot to pay the check.

Once my father sent me to the train station to try to catch up with him as he was leaving town. Welles put a pack of traveler's checks in my hand, and the train started to pull out. "Tell your father to sign my name," he shouted from the window. I can still hear his laugh, which he accomplished without removing the cigar from his mouth. It stifled the sound of the wheels until the train left the station.

In later years, I also remember Truman Capote, who always insisted on being served by the same waiter, Angelo Dal Maschio, an outstanding maître d'. He was an exuberant fellow but always consummately professional. "A-angeloo!" Capote would call out in that slightly affected voice as soon as he opened the door to Harry's Bar. It always had to be Angelo because Capote refused to think about what to order. Angelo ordered the author's food and drink for him. Whatever Angelo recommended was sure to be marvelous, said Capote.

Behind Truman Capote's seeming air of vague boredom, his eagle eye took in everything. I was surprised when he wrote with astonishing detail about the sandwiches at Harry's Bar in a newspaper article while sailing along the Yugoslav coast on Gianni Agnelli's yacht. According to him, the most interesting and important part of the cruise was the return to Harry's Bar for shrimp sandwiches.

Harry's Bar attracted many world celebrities of all kinds, from aristocrats to famous artists.

The Aga Khan was an important customer in the 1950s. A small man, not too rotund, very kind, very sweet, the Aga Khan was always asking everyone else in Harry's Bar if they were having a good time. Venice is not the ideal city for someone like him, who had difficulty walking, but he loved it nevertheless. The first time he visited he stayed at the Grand Hotel but immediately moved to the Bauer Grünwald; his justification was that it was closer to Harry's Bar. He could easily go back and forth between Harry's and the hotel by wheelchair without having to cross any bridges.

He always ordered the same things: beluga caviar to start, then *ravioli alla piemontése*. And the begum was always by his side. She was the only customer my father spoke of with enthusiasm, and it was clear that he had a secret admiration for her beauty.

Right outside Harry's Bar, the Chilean millionaire Arturo Lopez, the guano king, anchored his yachts regularly. The yachts exuded wealth but without a trace of ostentation. Lopez would rent an entire floor at the Grand Hotel, where furniture from his Paris apartment would be installed the week before his arrival, but he preferred to sleep on the yacht. He had afternoon tea at the Grand Hotel and dined at Harry's every evening. There were about twenty people in his entourage, and they had to adjust to the caprices of his mood. If he drank, everyone drank. If he was in the mood for water, it was water for everyone.

He always wore an impeccable dinner jacket and amused himself by touring the tables, asking the customers how they were enjoying their dinner and if they were satisfied with the service. So I would inevitably have to explain to the people, whose curiosity had been aroused, that the extremely polite gentleman who came on like a maître d' was the owner of the yacht outside the window. His daily tip was always exactly the same amount as his bill.

One evening just after Mr. Lopez had arrived, an old retired gondolier walked into the restaurant. As a way of earning small tips to supplement his pension, he used to stand every evening on the canal in front of Harry's Bar and help boats approach the shore with an iron hook.

That evening the gondolier showed me a ten-thousand-lire bill, a brand-new crisp banknote. He had never seen a bill of that denomination before. It would be worth about a hundred dollars today. Mr. Lopez had just given it to him.

As Mr. Lopez was leaving Harry's Bar that evening, he said, "Poor fellow, that gondolier, he has cancer and he still has to work!" On the gondolier's cap was written GANZER, the word in Venetian dialect for a hook man, and Mr. Lopez had mistaken it for a sign that the gondolier was suffering from cancer. I nodded in sympathy, and for the rest of Mr. Lopez's stay in Venice, every night the gondolier happily and uncomprehendingly received ten thousand lire from generous Mr. Lopez.

Of the countless millionaires who visited Harry's Bar, I remember Barbara Hutton. One of her many husbands was the famous tennis player, Gottfried von Cramm. She had married him in 1955, or rather, she had in effect married von Cramm and his entire entourage of some fifty people. She was an unhappy woman and drowned her sorrows in alcohol from morning till night. Von Cramm was homosexual, and his crowd was quite particular. She decided to give a big party at Torcello and asked me to decorate the island with ten thousand balloons. When it came time to pay the bill, she too was extremely generous and did not want to forget a soul; her total tips exceeded the bill itself.

Paying her husband's bills at the bar, however,

was another matter. She would pay them only if I
countersigned them.

Venice's beautiful port has historically attracted yachts
and boats of all kinds. Aristotle Onassis's yacht, the
Christina, was bigger than anyone else's. Onassis was
extremely rich, but he was no gentleman, as we all
discovered from the indiscretions of Elsa Maxwell, who
piloted him around Venice one summer. The famous gossip columnist was intelligent, perfidious, and extremely
acute, and she could be very ugly when she talked about
the people she knew. It was in Venice, between the yacht
and Harry's Bar, that the romance of Onassis and Maria
Callas began.

The *locanda* on Torcello is the only restaurant that Queen
Elizabeth II ever visited in a private capacity. That was
in 1960. She came to Italy on an official visit, and after
Rome she boarded the royal yacht *Britannia* at Ancona
and sailed to Venice. Her husband, the Duke of Edinburgh, had earlier been a customer of Harry's Bar when
he served in the British navy. Two months before the
royal visit, we received a letter from the court requesting
that we suggest a menu for a lunch the queen would
attend. We proposed and sent three, and all three were
accepted. They were simple dishes from our kitchen: ravioli, fried fish, pasta and beans, risotto with vegetables.
During the weeks preceding the visit, we became

the objects of several relatively veiled attacks from some of our competitors. The one that found the Torcello choice hardest to accept was the management of a major hotel chain whose generous offer of free lodgings had been politely declined by Buckingham Palace.

Despite the queen's wishes that the restaurant operate normally, the Italian authorities, for obvious security reasons, would not allow any unidentified parties in the restaurant that day. We invited several acquaintances who, while dining at our expense, were delighted to play the part of ordinary customers, as if they were walk-ons for a movie. My father was beaming when the queen told him how pleased she was by the way everything had worked out. She struck me as an extremely simple, reserved woman with a very sweet smile — in marked contrast to the noisy good humor of her husband. As she left the restaurant she walked over to my father and gave him, as a mark of gratitude, a beautiful pair of gold cuff links with the royal crest.

The countess Morosini had the most remarkably selective sense of hearing. "What beautiful eggs, Cipriani," she called out once as she entered the kitchen at Harry's Bar. "Look at the color of the fish, and what a joy this cake is!" My father had package after package wrapped up for her to take home. When we cautiously reminded her that there was a small bill to be paid, she replied, "What? I can't hear you, I don't understand," as if she had suddenly gone deaf. But if she was told that someone had left a gift for her, her hearing was perfect.

She often went to the casino; she loved playing cards. And her authoritative air, like her former startling beauty, was commanding and undeniable. Occasionally when the other players had paid to "see" and the hand was over, she would say, as dry as dust, "full house" and expect them to take her word for it. It worked well for her.

Hemingway once asked my father to send the countess a pound of beluga caviar with his compliments. The next day at cocktail time, la Morosini, as everyone in Venice referred to her, walked into Harry's Bar and ordered a drink. Then she called for my father. "Cipriani," she said, "I have a pound of caviar. I can't possibly eat all that. I want to sell it. What will you give me?"

She once sent a friend of hers, who had just married, a beautiful chandelier with her congratulations. The note she got back from him was not quite what she expected. "Thank you very much for the beautiful gift, but when I gave it to you, there were two."

A few years after the war, an enormous American man with a pleasant, ruddy face and a huge cowboy hat walked into the bar. Harry's Bar must have been his last stop on a long round of other bars in the city. He was in those rather loud high spirits that come from abundant drinking. He had enormous hands, and you could tell that he was as strong as an ox. With his ten-gallon hat shading his face, he took a seat at the bar, towering over all the other customers.

He brought a picturesque touch of color to the scene, but I realized at once that for Princess Aspasia of Greece, who was sitting by herself at a corner table, he incarnated an offensive symbol of bad manners. The princess started giving signs of alarmed disquiet. She shifted in her chair, sighed, and then signaled me over to her.

"Cipriani," she called out.

I went over to her table.

"Cipriani, have that boor take off his hat."

Had she asked me to move Everest a couple a feet, it would probably have seemed a more reasonable request.

I tried to reassure her and suggested that wearing a hat at a bar was probably conventional behavior in America. But there was no convincing her. Her purpose in life at that very moment was to get that damned hat off that guy, who, in the meantime, and despite my efforts, had realized that for some reason or other he was the subject of our conversation. He fixed an inquiring eye on the two of us.

"If you don't tell him, I will," Her Highness said. So I reluctantly headed for the bar, and I had the oddest sensation that I was growing smaller with every step while the American got bigger and bigger.

"Pardon me," I said in a hesitant voice, "it makes no difference to me personally, but the lady would like you to remove your hat."

"Why?" he asked.

I didn't dream of teaching him manners, so I lied: "The lady is allergic to hats!"

He turned to face the princess, gripped the broad brim of his hat in both hands, and pulled the hat farther down over his eyes. And not content with that, he got up and went over to sit down at her table.

It was a tense moment. But after a second or two of silence — while he looked at her and she felt embarrassed — he broke out in a sonorous laugh and removed his hat. The air suddenly cleared, and the princess laughed as well. The upshot of the whole thing was that they spent the rest of the evening wining and dining at the same table. When they finally walked out of Harry's Bar, I doubt that hats were even on her mind.

Princess Aspasia's daughter, Queen Alexandra of Yugoslavia, was the customer who caused us the most worry in those years.

Alexandra was very young when she married King Peter of Yugoslavia, a king without a throne, since he had gone into exile when still a child. After the king's early death in New York, the queen had become anorexic to spite her mother. When the two women went to restaurants, the daughter insisted on being served first since she was a queen, and her mother was merely a princess. We were all obliged to address her as Your Majesty.

When her mother died, Queen Alexandra made several suicide attempts. But with each attempt, she always made sure that someone took notice in time. Nevertheless, a couple of times she almost succeeded; one of these was at the Hotel Cipriani, the hotel and restaurant my father had founded on the island of Giudecca in 1953. She always took her swim in the hotel pool very early in the morning, so that no one would see her skeletal body. By chance that day my father had to be at the hotel at seven in the morning. Passing by the pool he saw the queen swimming. He summoned the pool attendant and, as if he sensed what might happen, told him: "Keep an eye on the queen today. I have a feeling she might try to drown herself."

Half an hour later the attendant lost sight of the queen. He went to the edge of the pool and saw her body stretched out at the bottom. He dived into the water and got her out in time. She was so thin that all she had to do was stay motionless and she sank at once.

Another time Alexandra wrote a letter with her last wishes to Count Paul Münster, who lived across the way from her on the Giudecca, and delivered it herself. She handed it to the maid and told her to give it to the count at once. Then she went back home and took thirty sleeping pills. But the maid was unable to deliver the letter, because the count had already set off for an all-day excursion. He only read the letter that evening on his return. They rushed over to her villa and were able to get her to the hospital in time. That one was a very close call.

The last two or three years of her life — this was in the 1980s — her mind no longer worked. Quarantotti Gambini, a lawyer, and I looked after her. She came to

Harry's Bar almost every day for lunch, and I made sure she ate.

Her son made it a point not to come to Venice to see his mother or pay her bills. She lived in her own apartment for a while, but she was finally obliged to move to an extremely respectable hospice. Things did not go well there either. In protest, she would stuff toilet paper in the toilet bowl until it was backed up. The plumbers had to be called several times. Finally — she must have been in her mid-sixties — the administration asked her to leave. I saw her off, with all kinds of advice. A car took her to Switzerland, where we had arranged for some faithful Yugoslavians to place her in a nursing home.

We all thought we would never see her again, but a few days later, to my surprise, she walked into Harry's Bar. "What on earth had brought her back to Venice?" I asked her. "I had to go to the hairdresser," she said. She ultimately moved to London and spent the last years of her troubled life there.

Despite the fact that her life was a very sad tale, she could be the most charming woman — simple, gay, and full of humor — especially after a couple of cocktails. Perhaps what she missed most of all was a normal life.

Among the strange customers I have seen, there was one who could sleep with his eyes open. That was Count Gozzi, an elderly Venetian nobleman who had bestowed his title on Mrs. Lee, the American woman who owned the Fortuny fabric factory. On her marriage she became Countess Gozzi Lee. She was an extremely energetic woman, but very boring. Listening to her for more than a minute left you helpless. To defend himself from the awful boredom of listening to her, Count Gozzi simply refused to speak English for ten years. When they brought guests to dine at Harry's Bar, almost always Americans, he looked straight ahead in a self-hypnotic state. I would set a dish in front of him and then give him a gentle nudge to rouse him from his trance. He never woke brusquely. On the contrary, he simply raised his fork and began eating slowly.

As all restaurateurs will attest, our profession makes us vulnerable to all manner of human encounter. I remember another odd customer, an aged Milanese *commendatore*. In the summer he would appear regularly about seven in the evening for an aperitif. He sat at a tiny table that I always set aside for him in the midst of the bustle of other customers. No sooner was he seated than he would almost immediately fall fast asleep. He usually slept undisturbed about twenty minutes. Then he woke up from his short nap, drank, paid, said thank you, and left. He finally confessed that he suffered from insomnia, and Harry's Bar was the only place he could sleep in peace.

And who could ever forget the fashion designer Valentina Schlee? She was of Russian descent and made clothes for Greta Garbo. They lived in the same apartment building in New York, and Garbo later became her husband's lover. Valentina always dressed like Greta Garbo, or rather, Garbo always dressed like her. Valentina always wore large hats to hide her face, even in summer. She was the joy and the sorrow of the cooks at Harry's Bar and at the Hotel Gritti, where she usually stayed.

She was extremely spoiled, and perhaps a bit mad. She was called the czarina in Venice, because in everyone's mind she seemed more suited to a czar's court than to the normal world. Obsessed about dieting, she would order pasta with no seasoning at all. The dish that reached her table, of course, was something on the order of library paste, and she regularly sent it back to the kitchen. When I was the one taking her order I would tell the cook to add just a touch of vegetable oil. Nobody would be able to tell, and the pasta would be excellent. She was fully satisfied and declared that I was the only one who understood her.

She was always escorted by an extremely polite gentleman named Barrett, a victim of her caprices. One evening the waiter failed to follow my orders and served the pasta the way she asked for it. I approached the table and had a glimpse of the pasta, which looked like a ball and was clearly inedible.

"How is the pasta?" I asked, turning to Mr. Barrett.

"It couldn't be lighter," Mr. Barrett gave a soothing smile, but started when she kicked him under the table.

Valentina absolutely refused to be served by certain waiters who, according to her, didn't show the right spirit as they transferred the food from the serving dish to the plates. And she was not altogether wrong. One day when she was in a particularly good humor, she explained that in gastronomy, the most important moment is when the food is served, because it has to sum up all the effort and artistry of everyone involved in getting that dish to the table, from the fisherman or farmer to the truck driver to the wholesaler and finally to the cook. She could not bear a distracted or indifferent air in the ceremony of service.

While theoretically she was right, each time she left, everyone heaved a sigh of relief. In a spirit of solidarity, I would send a bottle of champagne to the staff at the Gritti, to lighten the spirit of those who had served her there. Whether she was essentially good or bad at heart, she certainly had a strong personality.

7

HARRY'S GIFTS TO THE WORLD

H ARRY'S BAR AND MY FATHER'S INVENTIONS have left
their mark in many different and subtle ways, from the
carpaccio, which has become a generic term for thinly
sliced raw meat or raw fish, to the pink cocktail, the
bellini, not to mention his pale aqua Tiffany-like menus,
which have become our trademark.

In 1950 Venice was bedecked with red and white
banners: a major retrospective of the work of Vittore Carpaccio, the Renaissance painter, was being offered at the
Doge's Palace. The banners were in homage to the lumi-
nous red and white colors for which Carpaccio was justly
famous.

That fall one of the habitués of Harry's Bar, the

ravishing contessa Amalia Nani Mocenigo — one of my father's favorites — came in for lunch. She beckoned him to her table and informed him with tears in her eyes that her doctor had just warned her that she must go on a strict diet. For the next several weeks she could not eat any cooked meat. Could my father come to her rescue and dream up a dish that would be not only tolerable under these intolerable conditions, but hopefully delicious? My father smiled, acknowledging the challenge, and offered her a bellini.

Never at a loss, he said, "Give me fifteen minutes," and with that vanished into the kitchen. Fifteen minutes later to the minute he reappeared, followed by the maître d' carrying a beautiful fanlike display of paper-thin sheets of raw filet mignon, onto which was laced a white sauce that consisted of mayonnaise and mustard. "And what is that?" she asked. "A beef carpaccio," my father answered, as if the dish had existed for centuries, whereas in fact he had just made it up. Inspired by Carpaccio's red-and-white paintings, which like most Venetians worthy of the name he had visited and admired at the Doge's Palace, my father had on the spot combined a beef tenderloin with a white sauce.

Today imitations of carpaccio can be found in thousands of fine restaurants around the world, from Paris to New York to Tokyo. What the world doesn't know is that if my father had been a bit more egotistical, or as we would say today "PR oriented," the famous dish could just as fairly have been called Cipriani.

In creating what was to become known as the bellini cocktail in 1948, my father was once again inspired by a painter. The fifteenth-century Venetian painter Giovanni Bellini was often mentioned at home. I had no idea at the time that the pink glow my father had so admired in one of Bellini's paintings would be the inspiration for his famous cocktail.

Peaches are in abundance throughout Italy from June through September, and my father had a predilection for the white ones. So much so, in fact, that he kept wondering whether there was a way to transform this magic fragrance into a drink he could offer at Harry's Bar. He experimented by pureeing small white peaches and adding some *prosecco* (Italian champagne). Those who tested this new concoction gave it rave reviews, and my father was encouraged to pursue his alchemy. He named it the bellini, and from that day on the pink champagne drink became part of the Harry's Bar culture. For many years, in the kitchen of Harry's Bar, there were those whose sole function was to create the puree by actually squeezing and pitting the small and fragrant fruit with their hands. A labor of love. But because we depended on the peach season for fresh fruit, we could make the bellini only during these four months. Since then, an entrepreneurial fellow Frenchman has made his fortune by setting up a business that fresh-freezes the white peach puree, which he ships to me on an ongoing basis both in Venice and in New York — and also in Argentina, where a new Harry Cipriani has recently opened.

The popularity of the bellini was such that in

1990, somewhat against my better judgment, a Mr. Canella persuaded me to license the bellini to him. While it seemed a fine idea at the outset, it turned out to be one of my great errors. It was to be a "ready mix" containing the puree and the *prosecco*. And to accentuate the pink, he used a drop of raspberry juice. The drink was terrible. I was angry at myself for insulting the wonderful cocktail my father had created and soon confronted the licensee. His concoction was maligning the drink, its name, and Harry's Bar. In 1995 we took it to arbitration, I won, and the whole affair was promptly forgotten.

So the bellini reverted to its original, pristine state, saved from possible extinction by an arbiter's common sense and good judgment.

8

A TAVOLA!

THE FIRST TABLE THAT I REMEMBER with a particular pleasure is the one my family labeled the low table, where we children were confined during important meals. This table, besides being lower than that of the adults so that it was possible to sit around it by using the small chairs of our playroom, had the fundamental characteristic of allowing an almost absolute freedom, since we were far away from the scrutiny of my mother, who, with her primordial fear of hunger, used to stuff us with food during our daily meals. This low table was so called to distinguish it from the tall one where the adults discoursed on a high level, which to us children was incomprehensible at the time. There, we would not have been allowed to sprint to our seats as soon as we heard the call "*a tavola*," nor to prop our elbows on the table, nor to reduce the distance between the food and our mouths to an efficient minimum by slumping forward, unbridled and happy, as we did at the small table. There, at the most, we received looks of disapproval from my father, who could not get up to give us a well-deserved slap on the head because of the guests.

To return to what I consider the comfort of a table, I think that several elements need be considered. For instance, its height is essential, not only to prevent the guest from having to raise his elbow too much when he eats, but also, and above all, in order to make him comfortable. Too high a table creates a material and psychological barrier among the people who are seated around it and makes it very difficult for ideas, feelings, and spontaneous emotions to be transmitted. An adequate chair would seem the remedy, but this is true only up to a point, because the chair's height must allow the soles of the feet to touch the floor. Furthermore, the angle between the thigh and the calf must never be above or below 90 degrees. If a man is seated on a chair, the table should be at the level of the navel.

Another important consideration in determining the right height of a table is the height of the ceiling above it. We do not want to be crushed by the vertical immensity of a room. In order to ensure the equilibrium of this proportion, in the two apparently identical rooms of Harry's Bar in Venice, the tables on the ground floor are lower than those on the first floor. There's only a foot

of difference between the two ceilings, but it still had to
be taken into account.

Then there is the primordial question of the
table's shape. Should it be square, rectangular, or round?

The square table in my opinion is probably the
worst since it creates a sharp division among the guests. It
should be used only for games, certainly not to eat. The
four cardinal points are opposed, and the same antago-
nism, as subconscious as it may be, is necessarily gen-
erated among the four people seated around it. When
there are just two people facing each other, the effort required to maintain visual contact through such an insur-
mountable barrier will undoubtedly produce digestive
and emotional difficulties.

A rectangular table is more suitable for adulterers
because, if it is not too wide, it will be relatively easy to
touch the foot of a lover who is seated in front of us. If the
lover is seated beside us, we can still press our knee dis-
creetly against hers and get a mute but concrete promise
in return.

As enjoyable as these secret messages under the
table may be, they are not always as effective a means
of communication as one would like. I remember that
one evening my wife started to kick her neighbor at the
table, thinking she was kicking me; she was trying to
prevent me from telling a bit of anonymous gossip I'd
just heard that actually concerned our charming hostess.
I only found that out too late, on our way back home. I
also remember a dinner that was ruined when one husband, who knew that his wife was having an affair, saw

a woman's foot nestled seductively between the legs of the friend seated beside him. Thinking that it belonged to his wife, who was sitting in front of him, he jumped up, stared at her, and said, "Don't you think this is going a bit too far!" On the contrary, it was soon established for the benefit of all present that the innocent owner of the guilty extremity was the wife of the man's friend, who was also seated in front of him. Therefore, I do not trust rectangular tables because they can be the origin of countless unpleasant misunderstandings. And if they are long and narrow, they do not favor the conversation among those who are seated along the same side.

It would seem therefore that the perfect table is the one with the most natural shape: round, like the form of the universe. A round table is also the only one that can be made to stand firmly on any floor. For years, my father had the hardest time keeping the tables from wobbling. He eventually discovered that he could solve the problem if he took away one of the four legs and arranged them like a triangle instead of a square. But only a round table can have three legs. Moreover, this shape eliminates priority problems among the guests. I remember the dinner organized at the Doge's Palace in Venice for the conference of the industrialized nations. The presidents of seven states were present, and the only possible table that would have avoided antagonisms of etiquette was the round one. It is the table of equality, in which corners are replaced with calm curves. It is not by chance that it was chosen by King Arthur for his knights.

A TAVOLA!

I am always surprised that the world's most able diplomats keep forgetting the advantages of a round table. We all remember the distressing images of the long rectangular table during the negotiations between North and South Korea. The northerners were seated on the north side, and the southerners on the south. They were trying to negotiate an armistice, which was reached only after years of long and endless discussions and denials because, I am sure, of that table.

The size of a table, on the other hand, is less important than its shape, except that when you have a small number of guests, the wider their table is, the more they will have to raise their voices in order to be heard. The new czars of restaurant design, the acousticians, never tire of reminding us of this simple fact when they sing the praises of the small table, and in this one instance they are right. I believe that, starting from the presupposition that people — as I have said previously — absolutely need companionship not only to live, but also to eat, it is a good thing (and not only good, and deeply human, but also profitable for an innkeeper who needs to make maximum use of the space available to him) to place them as close together as possible. This way they can eat, laugh, joke, even touch each other a little with their elbows, and do everything that's natural to feel alive and present without making a show of it.

But on the whole I would send the acousticians back to their soundproof booths where they belong. Some claim that a man who dines should be able to enjoy the calm and tranquillity of a semidark and silent room.

Undoubtedly this is good for an ecclesiastic retreat or for a high mass. But personally, I do not like silence or indirect lighting or the excessive and onanistic obsession with the scarcely audible vibrations of the papillae on the tongue. I believe in the Dionysus, and in free spirit, and that man must be allowed every honest enthusiasm.

If, as we have seen, the shape and size of each table deserves the most careful attention, equally important are the quality and color of its natural ornament: the tablecloth.

I like to sleep and eat with very fine linen. Perhaps it is an indulgence on my part, but I think it is one I share with most people. The color of the tablecloth is crucial, of course, if only for the reason that it is reflected in people's faces. You will never find a beautiful woman who can sit calmly at a table with a green tablecloth, because instinctively she will realize that the green is bound to reappear on her beautiful complexion. On the other hand, pink will not go well with the purple color of her gallant companion, because at the end of the meal, he will seem more prone to a stroke than to a serene digestion. A pale yellow and ivory are the colors that I prefer, because they confer a pleasant clarity onto the surroundings.

I often think of the lace tablecloths that thousands of women from Burano have patiently embroidered for centuries — tablecloths on which they would never eat, objects that are splendid and marvelous because of the millions of stitches made by hand and woven with imagination. I wonder how many historical pronouncements have been made by heads of state on the wings of one of these embroidered butterflies.

As for the shape and color of the glasses, they deserve a whole treatise all to themselves. Two years ago I remember seeing some small glass amphorae at the Museum of Gallo-Roman Civilization in Lyons, France. Their exquisite lightness, which complemented their very pale blue color, made me breathless. Seeing them, I was confirmed in my belief that in matters of taste, there is nothing new under the sun, even though industry has progressed all these years. To hold in one's hand one of the slender octagonal glasses that were blown by the masters of Murano is always a thrilling experience, and to drink from it offers a moment of ecstasy.

In choosing a glass, balance is paramount, followed by color, which must be transparent. In order to be appreciated in all its spheric essence, wine must be looked at naked, like a beautiful woman. Then comes the rim, which must be as thin as possible, as is the case with coffee cups and demitasses. I do not like excesses in the size of a glass, since most often this is only a matter of showing off the virtuosity of the glassblower, and the shape must always be round. All the different shapes, colors, and artistic etchings that can be found in glasses undoubtedly reach remarkable formal effects, but in my opinion such glasses are not suitable for daily use.

Dishes that are disproportionately large always aim at hiding the poverty of what is being served. Not to mention the fashionable exaggerations by which the forms and the colors of a course are presented only as a decoration of the dish itself, regardless of substance. Dishes must contain the food in its various forms, and they serve just this purpose. Appropriate size to everything, sober and elegant decoration of the rim, and never of the center, which I prefer to be white.

My father revolutionized the choice of silverware in his establishments. After having gained experience in the great French and Italian hotels, he realized that, in many cases, the excessive number of forks and knives placed on the table served only as a cause of shyness and confusion among the guests. Where is the person who, at a gala dinner, has never peered up to see what his neighbor was doing before taking the right silverware in hand? Moreover, the knives and forks, not to mention spoons, that are designed to be used with the main courses are undoubtedly too large and heavy. Because of this, my father decided to set the table for his clients only with the silverware that is usually used for the dessert. And he always used only two pieces, a knife and a fork, which were of course changed for every course.

Silverware for fish seems to deserve special treatment, but it is not true that the knives and forks designed especially for this purpose are more suitable than the normal ones to separate the meat from the fishbones. In earlier days, before the invention of stainless steel, special silverware was used because knife blades tended to turn black when they were put in contact with lemon juice or wine.

In fact, from the very beginning the history of silverware has been plagued by an anxiety of decorum that has produced the most nonsensical aberrations. From Adam to the year 1633 everybody used his hands, then Charles I of England imposed the use of forks. Now we have entered the modern age, and perhaps we can at last agree not to confuse the technical limitations of the past with the truly immutable principles of classical form.

But all the attention paid to tables, chairs, and tableware will not make up for any flaw in what constitutes the true soul of a great restaurant: the people who sit at those tables, commonly known by us restaurateurs as the clientele.

The clients of a restaurant are divided, more or less, into two categories, according to the function of the table they sit at: those who "make" the table, and those who need a table to feel important.

The main motivation of the clients belonging to the first category is to enjoy to the maximum all the positive things that their chosen restaurant can offer. Therefore, they do not care much about the table's location. Before the enlargement of Harry's Bar in 1960, I remember we were often patronized by a very rich Parisian banker who never refused a table, no matter how crowded we were, how poorly placed the table. One evening he ate in the middle of the service entrance without complaining. He calmly ate his dinner with his wife sitting next to him, surrounded by the confusion of the waiters, the cooks, and the busboys who were rushing by with trays piled high with dishes and glasses.

But it is an unfortunate truth of the restaurant business that such clients are rare, and that those who need a particular table to feel important are a vast majority. The widowed wife of that same Parisian banker demanded, and still demands, to dine only if she is given a table in a corner. Anybody who wants to open a restaurant today would be well advised to shape the dining room like a star, as that is the only way to please all the customers who demand to be seated in a corner.

It has always seemed to me that, while the forces that move the heavenly bodies and everything else in the universe are many and mysterious, there are basically two forces that motivate people: luxury and snobbishness. And there is no better place in the world to see the difference between these alternating impulses than in a restaurant.

After years of careful observation, I have come to the conclusion that snobbishness can flourish only in times of great affluence, while luxury appears in times of crisis as a source of equilibrium. Snobbishness consists of the desire for the superfluous and in the intentionally careless use of the things that we use every day. When it is allowed entrance into the world of gastronomy, it leads to the most absurd sets of priorities and generally means giving a lot of importance to things and very little importance to people. In fact, the snob always qualifies almost everything that is obvious and normal as "divine."

Luxury, on the other hand, is the quest for quality, and hence for what is rare. In contrast to the snobs,

View from the quay
of Piazza San Marco,
around the corner
from the entrance
to Harry's Bar.

A street scene near Harry's Bar.

The terrace of the Grand Hotel in Venice. "In addition to the Europa there was the Grand Hotel, the Danieli, and the Bauer Grünwald, all frequented by the same clientele, and I started to think: 'Why not open a bar, just like the hotel bars but in a *fondamenta* in Venice, an elegant bar, but one customers can enter without running into a gauntlet of porters in braided uniforms or passing through a splendid but intimidating reception hall?'" *(Foto Alinari)*

(Right and below) Harry's Bar near the Piazza San Marco. "I liked the location at once because it was at the end of a dead-end street that at the time had no bridge connecting it to Piazza San Marco. This meant that the customers would have to come there on purpose, and couldn't just stop in as they were passing by. That is the way I wanted it. To this day people have to come to Harry's Bar on purpose. And as if to emphasize this fact, we have no sign, only the name of the bar etched in the windowpanes."

The interior of Harry's Bar today. *(Photo by Walter Vogel)*

Left to right: Claudio, Gigi,
Valentino, and Lucio, the manager.
(Photo by Walter Vogel)

Arrigo (right) in the downstairs
dining room of Harry's Bar.

Arrigo with (from left to right) Valentino, Vittorio, Mario, Giuseppe, and Nevio.
(Photo © Interpress Photo s.n.c.)

The upstairs dining room. *(Foto Arici)*

Giuseppe Cipriani, circa 1927.

Harry Pickering, for whom Harry's Bar was named, with
Giuseppe Cipriani, circa 1933. *(Publiphoto)*

Giuseppe with Ernest Hemingway at the *locanda* guesthouse on Torcello in 1948.

"There is a nice photograph of Hemingway and my father, the two of them wearing enormous sombreros. My father is smiling in the picture, but Hemingway, with his gray beard, looks lost in a dream before a flood of empty glasses. My father and Hemingway had apparently emptied those glasses, and I remember that it took my father three days to recover from his hangover." *(Cameraphoto)*

Queen Elizabeth II with the Duke of Edinburgh on Torcello in 1960, where she dined at the *locanda*—the only restaurant she ever visited in a private capacity. *(Photocronache Olympia)*

The letter Queen Elizabeth had an aide write to Giuseppe Cipriani thanking him for his hospitality.

Waiters from the *locanda* on the island of Torcello.

Giuseppe Cipriani preparing a cocktail at Harry's Bar. "It is not true, for example, that the secret of a good barman is the strange concoctions he invents. If you discount the short-lived aberrations that unscrupulous bartenders invent in an effort to stir up a little profitable notoriety at the expense of their customers' stomachs, there are actually very few variations on the five possible starting points of any cocktail: gin, vodka, whiskey, cognac, and rum. The trick is to make the classic drinks well, and to fit them to the particular taste of the individual drinker." *(Centro Documentazione Mondadori)*

The Hotel Cipriani on
the island of Giudecca,
founded in 1953.

The garden of
the Hotel Cipriani.

"At the entrance to San Marco, just down the quay from Harry's Bar, stand the two twelfth-century columns that once served as a kind of city gate during the times when Venice was accessible only from the sea....It was here that criminals were executed until the mid eighteenth century. Even today, superstitious Venetians will not be seen walking between these two towers." *(Photo © 1989 by David Hamilton)*

Arrigo Cipriani (center left), black belt in karate. "People who hear that I'm a black belt are intrigued to know why, and how a slight, congenial Venetian saloonkeeper like me ever got involved in karate...."

After a hard day's work, it's time for Arrigo's midnight dinner.

those who seek luxury are interested not in the quality that can be found in things, but in the quality that only people know how to give.

I remember the 1970s as the decade of maximum snobbishness, a time that coincided, incidentally, with the rejection of the traditional Italian and French dishes. Those were the years of macrobiotics. It was said that the intestines could not function if one did not force down two or three heaping tablespoonsful of horrendous bran that had been swept up by some very sly farmers from the floors of their barns, and which were put in little plastic bags to be sold as the remedy for constipation. Sitting with resigned, almost transcendental smiles, the credulous victims of the bran dogma had scarcely enough energy to stand up at the conclusion of their so-called meals, which generally consisted of two grains of wild rice and a portion of buckwheat seasoned with soya.

As was to be expected, it wasn't long before the tyrants of gastronomy, the food critics, had sold their souls for a provocative headline and given their stamp of approval to this "nouvelle cuisine," and shortly afterward, the restaurants fell in step. Soon, dining out at a fashionable restaurant meant swallowing two peas in a prune sauce, a very thin slice of Hungarian goose liver, and two raw spinach leaves, served as a side dish on splendid Limoges dishes.

"Divine!" the snobs cried out. But in the evening they collapsed onto their beds in comalike sleeps, despite what they had been told by the Master Chan Zi, which was that on a diet of peas and spinach leaves they would have the stamina to make love thirty times a week. Master Chan Zi died shortly afterward, killed by a car in front of which he had fainted, crushed by fatigue, while he was crossing the street.

The fads of the 1970s ultimately made me realize that man is the most credulous among the planet's inhabitants. Omnivorous since the beginning of time, he is easily convinced that, for instance, meat and fish are terrible poisons that will cause sudden death the minute they are ingested. But you would have a hard time convincing a lion to eat only honey and yogurt by telling him that the meat of the gnu is indigestible.

But even at the height of their authority, the gurus of the nouvelle cuisine could not keep preaching a gospel that stood in such stark contradiction to all the five senses of man. So to make up for what the taste buds were lacking, they spent all their energy describing the way the food should look. This explains the appearance in restaurants of very expensive Limoges porcelain, which, above all, had the function of diverting the attention of the eater, whose palate was silently protesting the scantiness of the courses, from the substance of what he was eating. I remember once sitting with my wife at a table for two in a famous restaurant in the late seventies and calculating the cost of the table setting. Without considering the linens, I arrived at several thousand dollars. Then the food came. With the exception of the wine, every dish was a disaster.

Even the terrorism of the period was a form of snobbishness. Born out of affluence, it replaced the properly human quality of reasoning with bullets and pistols. But the hidden pretentiousness of the terrorists was known only to themselves, some of whom, I learned later, occasionally took their young initiates to eat at Harry's Bar.

Happily, the jig is up for the snobs of gastronomy, because the crisis they caused is leading us back to the quality of tradition. The French chef Paul Bocuse, an extraordinary cook who has always had an infallible sense for which way the wind is blowing, told me recently that he now feels free to lift the lids off his pots and let the rich aroma of his grandmother's sauces saturate the kitchen. Soon the snobs will no longer be fashionable and will be replaced by the unsightly, but much less bothersome, hordes of nouveaux riches. They will pick up the crumbs of snobbishness and pay exorbitant prices — to the great benefit of us restaurateurs.

Regardless of the fads, however, the snobs will continue to cause trouble when it comes to table reservations. It is part of their nature, and I would sooner try to teach the sun to revolve around the earth than teach the snobs to behave reasonably when they expect to be shown to a certain table.

One August afternoon a few years ago, a former cadet of the Venice Naval Academy came to Harry's Bar.

The school was noted for its stern discipline, and its students included the scions of Italy's best families, such as the Aostas, the Rattazzis, and the Colonnas. In the 1970s the sons of these illustrious families became habitués of Harry's Bar every Thursday and Saturday evening, their evenings of liberty.

The former cadet was named Longanesi, an extremely polite young man I was quite fond of. He came in that August afternoon and told me in great secrecy that he had become the personal secretary of Prince Rainier of Monaco, who would be coming to Venice that weekend in a strictly private capacity. He said the prince wanted to dine at Harry's Bar on Saturday evening but thought it advisable to reserve the table in the name of Longanesi. I took the reservation in Longanesi's name.

That was on Tuesday. I had plenty of time before Saturday rolled around to forget, which is something I often do, the particulars of the Longanesi table among the other reservations for Saturday evening. I ought to mention as well that a reservation at Harry's Bar usually means you have the right to a table, but it may not be ready on the dot. This is not an affectation but a practice necessitated by what ought to be a rule in our business: no matter what the circumstances, it is totally unacceptable to deny a customer a table. So it often happens that we accept more reservations than we have tables, which means, unfortunately, that some customers may have to wait at the bar until a table is free.

That Saturday night we were full to capacity, and at eight o'clock sharp, in came Mr. Longanesi with Prince Rainier right behind him. My forehead broke out in a cold sweat. I had completely forgotten Longanesi's secret, and there was not a free table in the place. At least in the main floor dining room. Then I remembered our dining room upstairs.

I told Mr. Longanesi that for reasons of security I had thought it advisable to set aside a table upstairs. And I rushed up the stairs like a streak, only to find that the last table had just been taken. I pulled myself together, put on a smile, and stopped the prince in the hallway to ask if he would mind waiting a minute at the bar. Ten minutes later the prince lost patience and left, followed by Mr. Longanesi, who threw me a glance of sad reproof.

To my dismay, I never saw him again.

This is what happens sometimes to people who are not used to Harry's Bar. It's not that we have a policy of making people wait, but I must confess that the whole issue of table reservations is often confusing enough to overwhelm even the best of us. There is something mysterious about it, almost unfathomable to the human mind, and I often find myself treating it more as a matter of faith than of knowledge. Just the other day one of our habitués came in unexpectedly after he'd been away on a long vacation and asked if he could have a table for lunch. There was none. But we told him there was, a statement that, as anyone who is worth his salt in this business will confirm, was not a lie but a prayer. And somehow, with a little waiting, a little rearranging, we found him a table.

It was a little miracle, the likes of which happen almost every day at Harry's Bar.

9

KARATE AND ME

PEOPLE WHO HEAR THAT I'M A BLACK BELT are intrigued to know why, and how, a slight, congenial Venetian saloonkeeper like me ever got involved in karate. Like many things in my life, this did not come about in any rational, normal way.

What is karate?

A perfect coordination of body and mind. The wonderful discovery that we have gestures concealed in our bodies until the very moment someone shows us how to perform them.

It is probably the most difficult thing that I have ever done, but studying karate changed my whole life.

At the age of thirty-five I began to feel a strange weight at the top of my stomach. I went to see several doctors. All of them pronounced me fit and healthy. They could find nothing wrong with me. I mean nothing *really* wrong, thus suggesting that something was wrong but that they had not really figured out what it was. Most agreed that my feeling of heaviness had to be blamed on the malfunction of my liver, even if the blood tests had not shown anything particularly odd about the level of my transamination.

They prescribed a cocktail of thirteen pills a day that I would have to swallow before and after every meal for the rest of my presumably short life.

Three months after this mad routine began, a man, whose name I later learned was Bruno de Michelis, came into Harry's Bar one night to have a drink. De Michelis, it turned out, was the karate champion of Italy. He sat at the bar, slowly sipping a whiskey sour, apparently paying little attention to what was going on around him. Even seated, he was the biggest man I had ever seen. And there was a calm air of detachment about him.

Intrigued, I asked about him, and upon learning who and what he was, I went over and introduced myself, but got no real reaction. After a while I asked him if he would give me karate lessons in his spare time. Rather annoyed, he looked over at me and said that if I really wanted to learn karate, I could find him in his dojo every afternoon from three to six.

The very next day I went and began what was probably the most extraordinary experience of my life. Bruno was standing in the middle of the room wearing a kimono that made him look even bigger and stronger than I had remembered. During his visit to Harry's Bar, he hadn't spoken much; here he did not say a word. Talking with gestures, he made me understand that the lesson had begun. For an hour I tried to make my arms and legs follow his movements. At the end of this incredible effort I was ready for the hospital. Never before had I attempted anything so hard.

A few months after my first lesson, we started to have physical contact. I got so beaten up that for a long time I did not dare get undressed in front of my wife, who would have asked me all sorts of questions about where I had gotten all those bruises!

But the point is, before many weeks of this physical training — and abuse! — had elapsed, my internal physical ailments miraculously disappeared.

A few years later Bruno de Michelis told me that during our first six months, he had tried to throw me out of his dojo by beating me up in a very special way. He didn't know me at the time. The only effective way to make me leave would have been to ask me politely to do so.

So I never left.

After he saw that no matter how much he beat up on me, I was never going to leave, he gave up and we became great friends. Three years later I got my black belt. Two years after that I became an instructor in his dojo. I ended up teaching karate to seventy youngsters. Two of them, Diana Luc and Chris Gonzales, became European champions in their specialty.

So, the moral of this story is, if ever you feel

a strange weight at the top of your stomach, and your friendly family doctor can't for the life of him—or her— figure out what it is, I suggest you not despair but repair to your nearest dojo. Becoming a black belt is so much better than becoming a patient.

10

NAMES AND FACES

FOR THE LIFE OF ME, I still don't know if you should remember people's names or their faces. I believe that names were one of God's many inventions, or rather one of his "foresights." I think he did it to avoid complications.

He started out by calling the first man Adam and the first woman Eve, rightly guessing that they would subsequently reproduce almost ad infinitum. He may also have had taxes in mind. How could people pay their taxes if they didn't have first and last names?

But I am still convinced that the label society pins on a man counts less than what he is really like inside. That is the reason why I have never made a concerted effort to remember my customers' names. I recognize them when I see them. I am delighted to welcome them after a long absence, but often I have no idea what their names are, because knowing their names doesn't change a thing. Feelings are transmitted and exchanged by words and by thought, not by name, rank, and serial number.

Besides, how can you ask someone you have known for fifteen or twenty years, "By the way, what's your name?"

True, I am often embarrassed, especially when someone gives me regards from another customer whose name also means nothing to me. I have to pretend to remember the name, because I do not want to be rude, and, besides, I know full well that I would recognize the man if I saw him, and that I would be very pleased to have his greetings from a friend.

I remember the day a man walked into Harry's Bar and said, "My name is Smith. My son said to say hello to you."

I thanked him warmly, but no bell rang in my head at the mention of the name.

A little later, after doing the round of the tables, I went back to Mr. Smith.

"You know," he said, "my son is working with Mastroianni in New York."

I replied that I was delighted to hear it.

"Pardon me, the name is Rocco Papaleo," Mr. Smith added.

I automatically held out my hand and said, "Pleased to meet you, my name is Cipriani."

He gave me a long glance full of reproof and

pity and then burst out: "That's the *title* of the film my son is working on."

I nearly fainted, but I managed to rush off to my office in a sweat. I did not dare go back out to the restaurant until Mr. Smith had finished his meal.

Despite such embarrassing moments, I remain convinced that names are not what count in the restaurant business. I was confirmed in this belief by what happened one morning at Harry's Bar during the Venice Film Festival.

Sitting at the bar was a very attractive young Venetian woman with long blond hair, one of whose many lovers had for a while included the director of the film festival. Her black toy poodle was sitting politely at her feet. And I was at the cash register.

Out of the corner of my eye I saw the director of the film festival open the door for his wife. The two of them walked in, and the poodle immediately recognized the man — his old friend and his mistress's companion. Without knowing the man's name, the dog honored him with the most frantic, enthusiastic, and passionate outburst of joy I have ever seen. *Icy* is the best word to describe the atmosphere that the little dog managed to create, unbeknownst to himself.

But among the habitués of Harry's Bar, there are two whose names I will never forget, because they taught us all something about civility and grace that I have treasured ever since.

For as long as I can remember, Mr. and Mrs. Wood were always the same, from long before the magnificent hostelry that was the Grand Hotel was shut down and sold to the regional government without a word of protest. They used to come to Venice every year in August, and around six o'clock in the evening, they would be out on the balcony of their large first-floor room to watch the noiseless traffic on the Grand Canal. And so it was for many years. After the Grand Hotel closed, they stayed at the Bauer and later at the Gritti. They always had lunch and dinner at Harry's Bar.

Mr. Wood died not too long ago at the age of ninety. Tall and elegant down to the smallest details, he was a man of simple tastes, and he observed things and people from behind his eyeglasses with great interest and a touch of shrewd humor. Mrs. Wood is a small woman. She has white hair, thinning now and gathered in a white veil. She dresses with great care, stands erect, and is very knowledgeable; and the authoritative way she has of speaking, her chin slightly tipped up, is softened by the nice kind eyes.

I knew that if they didn't come August second, it would be the third, and they always arrived in the morning — a habit that suggested civility. They took a delicate pleasure in finding the same small things each year, fixed points for calm reflection on past love and feelings and joys.

One winter morning, five years ago, someone

told me they were very ill. He was paralyzed, and she had one of those illnesses it is hard to recover from. I thought about them with the melancholy associated with things that pass forever. But one day the following summer, Mr. Wood appeared at the door sitting in a shiny wheelchair. "How do you like my new car, Cipriani?" He stood up, a little more bent than usual, and very determinedly walked to his table. She accompanied him of course, very thin and frail. She leaned on a large cane, the only purpose of which, I am sure, was to keep her from being blown away by the wind.

After that, they had more difficulty doing things, but they compensated by taking even greater care in their dress, often with a touch of coquettishness. Old age and paralysis became the favorite subject of Mr. Wood's quick, humorous sallies. One day we managed to get him and his wheelchair onto a crowded *vaporino*. As soon as we had secured him a place, I could see he wanted to tell me something. I leaned over and listened carefully, because he has a way of swallowing half his words, which makes it hard to understand him. "You look tired today, Cipriani," he said. "Would you like my chair?"

Once, I told the waiter to remove the ashtray from his table, "Mr. Wood doesn't smoke." "Not yet," he remarked. A friend commented, "You're looking good, Mr. Wood," and he replied, "I'm not looking." Mrs. Wood usually looked at him and laughed on these occasions. It was like a game, a secret understanding they had. He pretended to be slow to see the comic side and took his time before giving a hearty laugh.

But the main reason I can never forget Mr. and Mrs. Wood is something they did two or three years before he died. It was the only time in the whole history of Harry's Bar that everyone stopped talking and looked to see what was happening.

He arrived first, and although he was not yet confined to a wheelchair, it was hard for him to get to the table. Nevertheless he managed without help from anyone. She came a quarter of an hour later. When he saw her at the door, he gripped the arms of his chair and slowly rose to his feet. She came over and stood at the table as if she were waiting for something. Everyone in the place seemed to sense that these two magnificent old people were about to offer us a marvelous lesson in life.

Old Mr. and Mrs. Wood's lifeline was so slender that you could sense the overwhelming power of the spirit in every thing they did. And for a magic moment everyone's attention was on them. She turned her face up to him, and he bowed his head to give her the sweetest kiss on the cheek. Time and space stood still for an instant, but I wished they would have stopped forever, because I am sure that of all the thousands and millions of kisses ever given or received in all the lands and islands known to the world, this was without the shadow of a doubt one of the most special.

11

THE HOTEL CIPRIANI

IN 1953 MY FATHER BOUGHT A PIECE of abandoned land next to a dilapidated workyard on the island of Giudecca. The owner kept his pigs there to fatten them for salami. Anyone who thought it a suitable place for a hotel would have been considered a madman.

But my father often went there. He stood among the wild undergrowth and looked out at the broad calm lagoon. From where he stood, he could just see the tip of the island of San Giorgio to the left with its pink brick walls framing Palladio's magnificent architecture. He firmly believed it was a perfect spot for a hotel. Then as the years passed, the difficulty of finding funds gradually dampened his enthusiasm.

One November evening, when Harry's Bar was half empty, Lord Iveagh, the owner of Arthur Guinness,

Son & Co. Ltd., the famous Irish brewery, came to dine. In the course of conversation, my father told him about the piece of land on Giudecca Island and his idea of putting up a hotel there.

"Cipriani," Lord Iveagh said, "would you show me the place tomorrow?" Lord Iveagh was a grand old man: he was in love with Italy, its landscapes and its history. He had gradually developed a splendid holding in Asolo that also included the villa where the great actress Eleonora Duse had lived.

The next day the weather was awful. Everything was gray, cold, slightly foggy, and damp, but Lord Iveagh was undeterred. When the two men reached Giudecca you could hardly glimpse the lagoon, much less the island of San Giorgio. And it was so muddy no one could even walk around to see the place, except for Lord Iveagh, who, heaven knows why, always wore enormous shoes with studded leather soles. He didn't say a word as they made their way around the pig run. Nor did my father, who was already regretting the foolishness of having dragged the nobleman all the way there. Then Lord Iveagh turned to my father. "Good," he said. "Count me in."

My father could hardly believe his ears.

A company was immediately established. My father provided the site, the name, and his future work, while Lord Iveagh provided the money. Exactly sixteen months later, in 1958, the Hotel Cipriani opened its doors for the first time. The night before the inauguration party, there was still no fountain in the garden. It was hastily dug that very night, and the cement was still wet the next day when it was filled with water and gold fish. The hotel looked like a large Venetian house with three wings, one on the lagoon side, one toward San Giorgio, and the third facing San Marco, and the three wings were so named.

The Hotel Cipriani expressed all of my father's splendid, intelligent experience. It was the embodiment of luxury service — sincere people providing simple things — the exact opposite of snobbery, which is merely appearance and the semblance of people and things. For example, the hotel laundry ironed sheets of the purest Czech linen so perfectly that I still remember their fantastic crisp feel when I got into bed, on the rare occasions I slept there. The luxurious texture of the pressed linen was so exceptional that it was almost nicer to stay awake, to roll over with your eyes shut on the Scotch wool mattresses that my father opened up and fluffed twice a year.

He always welcomed arriving guests on the shore, and every day he would go around with the German housekeeper to check on all the rooms. The restaurant, of course, continued to require his exacting attention. It was the only eating establishment worthy of competing with Harry's Bar in all of Venice.

A couple of years later Lord Iveagh asked my father to rebuild a hotel on his property in Asolo, the Hotel Belvedere. So in 1962 the Hotel Villa Cipriani was inaugurated in Asolo, which my father managed but did not own. It was an immediate success, one more healthy offspring of the wonderfully fruitful partnership between Lord Iveagh and my father. Their collaboration soon developed into a solid bond that was broken only by Lord Iveagh's death in 1967.

Not long afterward, his heirs and the family's new administrators made it clear to my father that even if he worked for the rest of his life, he could never buy out the share of the Hotel Cipriani that the Guinness company held as a guarantee against the loan my father used to build the hotel. The gentlemen's agreement between my father and Lord Iveagh that each could buy out the other's 50 percent share in any of their joint ventures had been buried with the earthly remains of Lord Iveagh, the last truly noble man of his family with one exception: Paul Channon, member of Parliament and nephew on his mother's side. He too is a true gentleman.

So my father decided to sell his shares in the hotel at Asolo to the Guinness family, shares that represented 50 percent of the enterprise. He sold them in 1968 for the equivalent of $161,290.

Meanwhile Mr. Bernard Norfolk, who had looked after the Guinness family's interests for more than forty years, was replaced by Colin Bather, an aggressive young manager from the Shell Oil Corporation. Gossip had it that when he left Shell, Mr. Bather's colleagues at Shell celebrated for three days. The fact remains that not long after his arrival, all of Lord Iveagh's property in Asolo was put up for sale, not just the hotel but the marvelous villa of Eleonora Duse as well. Officially it was all sold for $130,000.

It didn't take long for Mr. Bather to convince the board of the Guinness corporation to sell off the Hotel Cipriani on Giudecca as well. There were two possible buyers, one a shipping company called Sea Containers and the other a very rich customer of mine who wanted it at all costs and who matched his rival's offer. Nevertheless, Mr. Bather preferred Sea Containers, because they promised him a seat on their board of directors. Our customer's bid included no such offer.

The president of Sea Containers then and now is a man named Jimmy Sherwood, a Texan. Enzo Cecconi, who was the manager of the hotel when it was sold, remembers him because his favorite meal was hamburgers, which he always ate with his hands.

Jimmy has a round face that looks as if it might have been waxed, and his head seems to sit, without the aid of a neck, directly on a body just as round as his face. The best definition I could give of Jimmy Sherwood is *Homo ridens* ("laughing man"). That is Jimmy to a T. He laughs — most of the time in the key of "eh." Of course, constant laughter may be common practice among some American tycoons; I've seen it often. But you don't usually expect a laugh in the course of serious conversation about the world's economic crisis. Jimmy Sherwood manages to laugh about anything, with quite an unsettling effect on anyone in the vicinity.

Moreover, Jimmy lives and acts on the basis of polls and market research. And he is always up on what will happen in the next ten years. When he bought the Hotel Cipriani, market research showed that the age of elegance was coming to an end, and that *posh* was the new byword.

Posh means furnishings. *Posh* means *épater le bourgeois*. Indeed, the more a bourgeois is intimidated by kitsch, the more he is willing to pay for it and, what is more, pay without daring to complain — for fear of looking like a fool. This was about 1968, the year of the revolution of the snobs. Jimmy immediately got in line with the new philosophy, not least because it was quite congenial to him. In no time everything at the hotel changed. And unfortunately, the polls were right: the idea worked.

Architects and decorators were called in. The dining room was judged too banal, so a new one was designed in imitation of the Basilica of San Marco. The bar took on a Caribbean air. And the poolside apartments were decorated after the fashion of the cabins on Kassoghy's yacht — with television sets that rose magically at the foot of the bed, and mirrors, mirrors everywhere. There were mirrors in which New Jersey druggists could proudly display their tanned faces and bodies and admire the reflection of their heavy gold necklaces and medals.

A round Jacuzzi tub was a must for the bathroom, and there were flowers, plants, trees, and forests everywhere.

The waiters were decked out in gondolier costumes summer and winter.

One July morning not long after the hotel was sold, I had breakfast there with some of my customers. It was hot. It looked as if fatigued gondoliers were rowing aimlessly around the garden. The maître d' came over to our table, his jacket unbuttoned. He proudly displayed a ghastly studded belt buckle under his protruding belly.

"What'll you have?" he asked in a tired voice as perspiration streamed down his forehead.

"Nothing from a maître d' who doesn't button his jacket," I replied.

No excuse was forthcoming, simply: "It's hot!"

"For everyone, or just for you?" I asked.

One of Jimmy's first decisions had been to replace the excellent Cecconi with a man named Natale Rusconi as manager-director. He chose Rusconi from among the available snobs because Rusconi had a particular way with journalists and PR people; a liking for old recipes modernized to guarantee acidity; and an almost incestuous love of his own ego. I remember him saying with a superior air, "The more they pay, the happier they are." It was his decision that the restaurant go overboard for the nouvelle cuisine.

Rusconi had been assistant director of the Gritti in the early sixties, under a Swiss director named Fred Laubi, who, in addition to having married an intemperate Ballantyne of the knitwear family, bore a dangerous resemblance to a hot dog. Shortly after he took over the Hotel Cipriani, Rusconi and his pal Laubi convinced a journalist who was living at the hotel at the time to put Harry's Bar on the "out" side of his "In and Out" column in *Town and Country*. Henry Sell, the magazine's editor at large as well as a treasured friend and admirer of Harry's Bar, immediately fired the misinformed scribe. I knew then that postfascism was around the corner.

Among the hotel's regular customers, the remarkable people who came every year to spend their vacation in this oasis that is Venice, there was a very old Belgian couple, the Boases. He was the quiet type, and she was classy, full of energy, and imbued with a keen sense of humor. Few women in the world, I think, can match the class of some Belgian women I have known.

They had lunch or dinner at Harry's Bar every day, but only one meal a day. The other meal they took at the Hotel Cipriani, where they were staying. One day they came in at lunchtime quite upset. Madame Boas was in tears, and he looked stunned. I asked what was the matter. With tears running down her cheeks, she told me that the evening before, after waiting twenty minutes to be served minestrone, she had gone to the table where the manager was dining with some journalists. She teasingly asked why the manager's table was served before hers. Her tone was bantering and friendly, the tone of an old customer who feels quite at home.

The response came the next morning in a letter from Natale Rusconi himself stating that the management accepted complaints at nine o'clock in the morning in the appropriate forum, namely, the manager's office, and that in any case the Boases should consider themselves unwelcome at the hotel in future.

I telephoned Jimmy at once and was informed

that no one was allowed to interfere with decisions of his manager, Natale Rusconi.

This deplorable story shows how the concept of service can be perverted when love is missing.

Yes, you need love to serve.

The Boases never came back to Venice, but it was a terrible blow for them. They had felt at home at Harry's Bar, just as they had at the Hotel Cipriani when my father ran the hotel.

I sometimes wonder if the incomparable gift of service, which arises from love and civility, has been lost forever. It would be an irreparable loss.

Another of Jimmy Sherwood's snob enterprises was the reconstruction of the Orient Express railway train. The purchase of the train carriages, on Mr. Bather's advice, at first seemed to be a great bargain. The rusty old carriages that still survived in railway depots around Europe cost some thirty thousand dollars each. Once purchased, the finest decorators familiar with the belle epoque style were called in for restoration work.

When the train was ready to go on the tracks, it became clear that the carriage wheels could not stand up to the speed of modern-day locomotives. So after the money spent on restoration, a total of more than four hundred thousand dollars went to the revamping of each carriage.

It is a fascinating train to look at, but there are no bathrooms or air conditioning. There are two toilet bowls for every twenty passengers. But each compartment has an elegant porcelain chamber pot all its own.

One day a customer remarked, "That Orient Express is incredible — I've taken it twice," and then with a wink, "the first time and the last."

Jimmy was relentless in his pursuit of image and even decided to copy Harry's Bar. He did it jointly with Mark Birley in London. But the only thing their restaurant has in common with Harry's Bar are the chairs and the name.

I discovered this when I was invited to London to give my seal of approval to the new enterprise. I suppose the owners wanted to impress me, because a white Rolls-Royce picked me up at the airport. I felt like a groom on his way to his wedding. But if they wanted to impress me, the Rolls was the wrong choice — a Ferrari is my car.

The next day an enormous sky blue Cadillac came to collect me at the Connaught Hotel — just about the only oasis of service left in the world among the hotels I know — to escort me to Mark's Club, as the restaurant is called, which must have been all of two blocks away. The striking young woman at the wheel looked something like a jaded majorette with white boots and enormous sky blue sunglasses. I honestly don't remember if her hair was blond or blue like her glasses, but it was certainly a pleasant enough experience. Outside the Connaught, I felt obliged to give the hotel porter a knowing wink to dissociate myself from this display of garishness. I felt as if I was on some kind of television soap opera.

Nothing came of the meeting, because I realized the only thing that interested them was using my name. My sister Carla was also invited to act as godmother at the opening, but she too declined the invitation. In the end, the part of godmother fell to the Venetian Afdera Franchetti, Henry Fonda's ex-wife.

12

HARRY'S FIFTH AVENUE

ONE DAY IN MAY 1985 LORD FORTE, the well-known British restaurant owner, called me from London. A few years before, my father had invited him and his wife home for lunch, when he was still only Mr. Charles Forte. I had seen him a couple of times subsequently at Harry's Bar. He was an extremely cordial man with very bright, foxy eyes. And so they should be.

The subject of his telephone call was an invitation to London to talk about opening a restaurant in New York. We made a date. First we met in his office, and then I was invited to lunch at his beautiful house, where I spent two delightful and amusing hours with him. His wife was there, her brother, their son Rocco, and if I am not mistaken, Forte's splendid daughter Olga, who had married the Italian Alessandro Polizzi di Sorrentino. Lord Forte talked a great deal during the meal, making a number of witty comments, not all of them appreciated by his guests.

"When I was young," he said at one point, "if I had a slight headache, my wife called four doctors. Now no sooner do I have a headache than a solicitor is called to make certain all the papers are properly signed." The smiles that greeted this remark were rather forced. He made a few remarks about his daughter, Mrs. Polizzi, too, but it was clear nevertheless that she was his favorite. She was the one whose mind was most like his.

He talked pleasantly about whatever came into his head, the way successful men do at a certain age, when they no longer have to worry about what other people think.

He and his son Rocco told me that the place they had in mind for the restaurant was a beautiful site on Fifth Avenue. Above the restaurant was an old hotel, the Sherry Netherland. Trusthouse Forte, as the Fortes' family business was called, had set its eyes on it. They wanted to open an outstanding restaurant on the main floor in hopes of persuading the owners of the building to let them take over the management of the hotel.

I demurred because I did not have the time, but Rocco persuaded me that I should at least go to New York to have a look. I vividly remember the trip, because it was the first time I set foot on board the Concorde, that

seagull of the air. I had been to New York only once before, and for one day only, stopping over on our way, my
wife and I, to Birmingham, Alabama, where my daughter was to have heart surgery. When I think back to that
first, fretful trip, I still remember how moved I was by
the incredible sight of the twin towers of the World Trade
Center, which were still under construction at the time. I
ascribed my emotion on that first trip to my fragile state
of mind, every thought centered on my daughter. But
this time I was truly overwhelmed by New York.

As soon as I saw the location the Fortes had
picked out, I knew it was perfect. That was the right
place for Harry's Bar of Venice to install its New York
cousin. The two big windows opened onto the plaza at
the end of Central Park, dividing Manhattan in two. It
was Sunday, and a crowd of people was listening to amateur bands playing Mississippi blues at the foot of the
golden statue. All around, the horse-drawn carriages patiently waited their turn. When I looked up, I reacted
no doubt as a thousand tourists had before me; my head
and stomach were violently struck by four or five elegant
skyscrapers that seemed to have nothing to do with life
below.

I wrote Rocco — he was the one who would be
managing the venture with me — giving him my terms.
I wanted to call the restaurant The Copy, but we finally
settled on Harry Cipriani. I absolutely would not call it
Harry's Bar. I was anxious to show all the people around
the world who had copied our name that names are not
what counts. What you have to copy is what is inside.

Soon after my communications with Rocco, an architect appeared in Venice to photograph and take the measurements of Harry's Bar. While I had not received an answer from Rocco, I concluded that silence meant consent. And construction work on the New York site began at once.

I went to New York again some time later, and my first impression was confirmed. There are ways to make a bar or a restaurant mirror its location. One way I learned from my father, namely, the total absence of constraints that might deprive the spirit of man of its free expression. And when those constraints are all removed, the place is no longer just a place to contain people but has emotions and feelings of its own. I knew that Harry Cipriani could be such a place.

My impressions about New York and about Americans in general, whom I had known in Venice for many years, were also confirmed.

About the skyscrapers of New York. Only a nation that earns a great deal of money can dare build structures that burst skyward. You might say that the height of the buildings is an index of a country's wealth. It is common knowledge that I have never had a soft spot for architects, but I must admit that height is precluded in Italy, not only because of lack of money but because of the authorities who supervise monuments. If an architect is forbidden to use one of the four dimensions, all that he can do is try to ruin Palladio and his buildings. So I acknowledge that it is much easier to practice architecture in New York than in Italy, because once you have designed the second floor, all you have to do is multiply that by the number of millions of dollars available.

Briskly walking down the Avenue of the Americas, between the sensational walls of gigantic buildings, I realized that I never felt small. That's what is remarkable about New York. In all its immensity, people do not lose their own dimension.

The construction of the restaurant went forward. A few days before we were to open — this was November 1985 — Rocco telephoned from London to say that my monetary demands were too high. They weren't. We argued back and forth. Deeply convinced that my demands were in fact reasonable, I offered not to go ahead. There was no need to proceed as far as I was concerned. It was too late to turn back, Rocco answered. By the time Cipriani on Fifth Avenue opened, we still had no written agreement. When, in 1985, we opened Cipriani's, we created a sensation.

From the very first days there was always a crowd of lively people, merrily sipping bellinis, chatting, and waiting at the bar for their tables. There were hundreds and hundreds of customers. And what was more, I knew every one of them. It was as if all the customers that came to Harry's Bar in Venice in a year had arranged to be together in New York at one time. For a good decade now, Harry's Bar's American cousin has enjoyed a consistently full house.

I worked sixteen hours a day, but I never felt tired, embraced as I was by an incredible sense of human warmth. To me, New York is not a city, but a feeling.

Just like Venice. New York and Venice: these are the only two places that to me are not cities but feelings. The replication of Venice's Harry's Bar was so perfect that during the first days of business on Fifth Avenue, the only way I could be sure I was actually in New York and not in Venice was to look out the two large windows on Fifth Avenue. The white lights moving outside were automobile headlights, I reassured myself, and not the lights of speedboats in Saint Mark's harbor. Because inside, the voices, the lighting, the soft hubbub of the customers, and the feeling of well-being were all identical with my Harry's Bar in Venice.

What made these two different and fantastic cities so much alike? I wondered. Could their asymmetry be one of the elements? Venice is asymmetrical by nature, but the asymmetry of New York is something created by people. While the layout of New York City is absolutely geometrical, there is an enormous asymmetry in the way the skyscrapers are situated in concentrated bundles. The towers of New York and the palaces of Venice express other kinds of asymmetry as well, the asymmetry of wealth and poverty, the asymmetry of the different races that have lived side by side, and continue to do so, and the asymmetry of so many contradictory sensations. The palaces on the Grand Canal represent the churches of powerful men, and in New York, I perceived the skyscrapers as stupendous obelisks reaching for the sky.

Every day I was struck by another similarity. The way you get around both cities is on foot. One city is, and the other one was, the trade capital of the known world. Wherever you live in either city, however, you realize you are in a neighborhood. In both places you find the little shop that sells buttons, the local grocer, the shoeshine parlor, and the shoe repair shop. If you walk the same streets at the same time every day, you cannot help but see the same faces, and after a while, however shyly, you start greeting them and being greeted in return.

Both cities are clearly defined by water.

The big difference to me is that New York moves at a faster pace than Venice does; it is more energetic and now richer.

While I concluded that New York in its own way shared a bit of Venice's charm, I also discovered similar flaws — such as snobbism.

At 12:30 on the dot one Sunday some weeks after we opened, a woman, perfectly turned out in Coco Chanel from head to foot with a tall, rather dandyish looking gentleman right behind her, entered through the revolving door of our restaurant. They hurried right by me, neither of them acknowledging my greeting. Her voice sounded highly professional as she gave her name to the maître d', who is second in command on Sundays and shares my views on the relative importance of tables and the people who sit at them.

We both had paid scant attention to the fact that the reservation for Mr. Pinkerton and his secretary had been made by a magazine that once was the height of fashion but was starting to slip. We offered them a table for two that was in a key position in terms of subtle sophistication. From that table you could see everything without being seen by anyone else.

We had been told that he wasn't merely a famous photographer, but the most famous photographer in the world. He did not dress like a photographer, though I have to admit that of all the famous photographers who have dined in our restaurants, none of them ever looked like any other. It is totally impossible to classify photographers, because they defy any known morphological system, at least in terms of the things a restaurateur notices. They range from the suppressed tumult of a Roiter to the Emilian singsong of a Fontana and the odd bouncy step of a Snowdon. Each one is different from the other.

I wondered whether Mr. Pinkerton specialized in fox hunting, because he dressed like an English country gentleman. He wore a beige wool jacket, and on top of that a very Sundayish cashmere sweater was slung over his shoulders and tied in front by the sleeves. He did not utter one word.

After a while I went over to them with a pleasant smile, but neither of them noticed me. He had sipped up the broth from his minestrone without touching the vegetables, and her full attention was engaged in moving the ravioli around her plate with the end of her fork. The atmosphere in the dining room around them was friendly, casual, and unconstricted. The only thing that was out of place was the hostility at that table for two. I asked in vain if everything was all right and got no answer, so I paid no further attention to them. In the end they skipped dessert and hastily asked for the check.

When they were at the door, she came over to me and said: "You'll regret having given Mr. Pinkerton that table!" Without waiting for an answer, she stepped into the revolving door behind him. But halfway through, she changed her mind and came back in. "You'll see," she said threateningly, "what we write about you in our magazine!" She went back to the revolving door and out into the sunlight of Fifth Avenue, leaving me speechless, and somewhat sad.

I thought a bit as I watched them leave and then returned to see how the other diners were doing. There was a young couple now at the table where the Pinkertons had been sitting, and they seemed to have a great desire to look into each other's eyes. They gave me a happy, reassuring smile in response to my interest. And I immediately felt at peace with myself.

Two months after the New York Cipriani restaurant opened, when even the Trusthouse Forte bookkeepers were convinced that it was a great success, Lord Forte telephoned: "Dear Arrigo," his voice was jolly, "my compliments, my warmest compliments."

"Thank you," I said, "but I am afraid my asking price was too low. My price has gone up."

This cooled his enthusiasm markedly. "All right, but don't overdo it!"

After I conveyed to him my firm position, he said: "I'll call you back in five minutes," and hung up.

Exactly five minutes later he called back. "All right, then. Keep up the good work."

A few days later my son Giuseppe took over the restaurant, and I returned to Venice.

Despite recession, snow blizzards, and other calamities, Cipriani of New York is packed each lunch and each dinner.

13

THE BELLINI

THE FIRST YEAR WE RAN HARRY CIPRIANI'S was punctuated by letters, communiqués, and little episodes that constantly showed the degree of irritation our success provoked in the wooden heads of the Trusthouse administration in the United States.

Meanwhile, the Forte family's hopes of taking over the management of the hotel above the restaurant became increasingly remote, because their representatives treated the landlords with crude arrogance that soon lost the Forte family's credibility and appeal. Every time the restaurant was mentioned in the papers, the Trusthouse Forte complained that their name was never mentioned.

After receiving an altogether idiotic letter from

the vice president of the Trusthouse Forte, I wrote in response:

> Dear Tom,
> Dear Tom,
> Dear Tom,
> I am speechless.
> Arrigo

I had no doubt, however, that his total lack of a sense of humor would prevent him from understanding my message.

In the meantime, not a day went by, during my stays in New York, that someone did not offer us a chance to open a new place. Among the many offers, one seemed worthy of attention. It was a site on the ground floor of an old hotel that was being restored, the Taft—now the Michelangelo—on Seventh Avenue in the heart of the theater district.

I telephoned Rocco to ask if the prospect might interest him. He responded affirmatively.

So I went ahead with negotiations until a few days before the agreement was to be signed. Rocco suddenly had changed his mind. He had thought things over and decided not to go ahead. This was early 1987. I signed the agreement on my own and soon found another partner willing to finance the enterprise.

At the end of May 1987 the Bellini was inaugurated—not without incident, as you will see in the next chapter—a handsome restaurant this time decorated like the second floor of Harry's Bar in Venice. Now, with the opening of the Bellini, I had *both* floors of the original Harry's Bar replicated in New York, which made me feel even more at home in my adopted city.

By July it was clear that my second New York restaurant had created a clientele of its own without interfering with the Harry Cipriani. But the rumor began to circulate among the Forte brains — as I learned only later — that the Harry Cipriani on Fifth Avenue could very well do without the Ciprianis. A secret plot was hatched to look for someone else to run the restaurant.

On August 31, 1987, the president of Trusthouse Forte America, a Mr. Combemale, an almost perfect imitation of a British dandy whose only claim to fame was having married a very rich and well-connected woman, summoned my son Giuseppe to the company's main office at three in the afternoon to inform him that at six o'clock that evening, a new manager would be replacing him.

Giuseppe, like his grandfather before him, has a capacity for seeing the funny side of things even in difficult moments. When he realized that it was no joke, he said "You'll have to drive us out at rifle point," and off he went.

He then telephoned me in Italy. At the very moment we were having our astounding conversation, about five in the afternoon New York time, a truck pulled up outside the Fifth Avenue door of the restaurant. Several men got out, wearing hats and double-breasted pin-striped suits. They went into the restaurant and, applying guerrilla — or was it gorilla? — strategy, took up their strategic positions. They blocked the telephones, the elevators, the kitchen, and the doors. Two of them flanked the director and followed his every move. The sign outside was taken down, and another one was put in its place. Harry Cipriani had a new name.

When my son Giuseppe arrived back to work at six o'clock he was prevented from entering the premises. Clearly the ineffable Mr. Combemale had taken Giuseppe's remark seriously.

After a shoving match, Giuseppe left.

This interesting episode seemed to me more like a story from Chicago in the thirties.

The next day, the front page of the *New York Times* carried the story of our departure: AT LUNCH: IT'S HARRY CIPRIANI. AT DINNER: IT'S TINO FONTANA, with a picture of me on the left and one of Tino Fontana on the right. This caught Trusthouse Forte off guard — they had planned a "painless" rebirth. What most struck Italian journalists in the days that followed was the lightning-quick succession of events. Press accounts often contained more fiction than fact. A couple of days later I took out a half-page ad in the *Times:*

DEATH IN THE AFTERNOON

Harry Cipriani announces the sudden demise of Harry Cipriani Restaurant. Its loving spirit and soul will remain forever at its brother restaurant, Bellini by

Cipriani. Trusthouse Forte, Inc., the holder of the lease to the Fifth Avenue location, decided without any notice to change the name of the restaurant and to grant the management of the restaurant to others.

Most of the sixty employees followed us to the Bellini on Seventh Avenue.

The Fortes installed a new manager in the Fifth Avenue restaurant named Tino Fontana, a totally unknown ice-cream vendor from Bergamo, the inventor, as Forte's PR people subsequently reported, of the "new modern Italian cuisine," a sort of incestuous liaison between the French nouvelle cuisine and the culinary idiocies of the post-1968 Italian extremists. It fell to him to orchestrate the long agony that ended in 1990, when the restaurant had to close for lack of customers.

A few months later, the landlords of the Sherry Netherland Hotel called and invited us to return. And the Harry Cipriani reopened in 1991. It was once again a triumph. The day we opened, it was as if all our old customers had been waiting the whole time in Central Park for our return. The reopening of Cipriani was one of the most touching and unforgettable moments of my life. I felt surrounded by the vivid, tangible, and warm affection of my friends in New York, a city where everything is possible, including great love. And I am forever grateful. Everything went well, and I shared my time between Venice and New York with my son Giuseppe and daughter Giovanna, who would spell me.

Then there was the taxi incident. It was said to be an omen, but it was not.

Jean Paul Spence, a Hawaiian taxi driver in New York, had just got his license back after a three-month suspension. About seven in the morning one Sunday in February 1992, after working all night, he was happily challenging the world free-flight taxi record by racing east along Fifty-ninth Street in the direction of Fifth Avenue at eighty miles an hour.

He thought he could beat the traffic light before it turned red, but he was wrong. So to avoid a car that was just crossing Fifty-ninth, he veered slightly to the left without slowing down, and smashed — in the following order — a municipal clock, a mailbox, and a plant in a large terra-cotta pot. Then he shot through the right window of the restaurant like a high-caliber bullet, reared up and struck the ceiling, came down heavily among the empty chairs and tables, grazed a reinforced concrete pillar, tore through three plasterboard walls, touched ground next to the coffee machine, and finally came to a stop, miraculously unharmed, against a very heavy steel refrigerator chock-full of bottles. As in a cartoon, he had in his taxi entered Cipriani and traversed about seventy-five feet of restaurant and done hundreds of thousands of dollars of damage within thirty seconds.

We reopened the restaurant five weeks later. I hung the hubcap and the taxi's license plate on the new back wall with the following inscription:

The February '92 renovation was sponsored by Jean
Paul Spence, a New York taxi driver, who left his license plate at the Harry Cipriani Restaurant early in
the morning of Sunday February 2nd 1992.

14

ONE DAY IN THE BUILDING OF THE BELLINI

WHAT DO HARRY'S BAR, the neighboring Piazza San Marco, and the late, lamented Bellini restaurant in New York City have in common? They all share a building history. Harry's Bar, from the time my mother found it till the time my father opened it, took three months to complete. Raw warehouse space to gleaming new restaurant without a hitch. Its neighbor, the Piazza San Marco, took a bit longer, of course, but in all fairness its story begins in the ninth century, roughly a millennium (give or take a century) before Harry's Bar opened.

The Piazza San Marco is named, as we are told

in school, after Mark the Evangelist, whose bodily remains were brought there from Alexandria in A.D. 829 after being stolen by a group of intrepid Venetians. According to legend, the relics were smuggled out under slices of pork. A church was built to house the relics but burned down in A.D. 976, taking all worldly trace of Saint Mark with it — or so it was believed for some nine hundred years, until the day the present Basilica of San Marco was consecrated after remodeling in 1904, when the remains were rediscovered miraculously on the very same spot they would have lain in the original church.

The Torre dell'Orologio, or Clock Tower, that has graced San Marco since the late 1400s also had a bloody birth. It seems that the inventors of the clock mechanism were rewarded for their labors by having their eyes gouged out to ensure they would not repeat their engineering feat for some competing European capital.

Another landmark of the square, the great Campanile tower, was originally built in the sixteenth century. One day in 1902, it collapsed without warning, killing the custodian's cat. Finding the sight of a decapitated Piazzo San Marco unbearable, the Venetians promptly took up a collection to finance the reconstruction of the tower "as it was, where it was," which was completed in 1912.

At the entrance to San Marco, just down the quay from Harry's Bar, stand the two twelfth-century columns that once served as a kind of city gate when Venice was accessible only from the sea. The architect of the columns, Nicolò Baratari, who also designed the first Rialto Bridge, was rewarded for his labors with a license to set up gambling tables between them. Later, the columns marked a less jolly sight, for it was here that criminals were executed until the mid-eighteenth century. Even today, superstitious Venetians will not be seen walking between these two towers.

But the heart of the piazza is, of course, the beautiful Doge's Palace, for centuries the only house in Venice that was honored with the name *palazzo*, all other dwellings being relegated to the class of the *casa*, "house," or *ca'* for short. Built in the fourteenth century and completely remodeled over the next four hundred years, the palace has a beautiful white-and-pink marble façade. What went on inside was not always so cheery. It was here, in the Room of the Cord, that suspects were interrogated while hanging from their wrists. Those who were found guilty were led over the Bridge of Sighs, so named because prisoners were heard to sigh as they glimpsed their last ray of sunlight before disappearing into the prison across the canal.

It took about twelve workmen three months to complete Harry's Bar. It took hundreds if not thousands of masons and master carpenters and roofers to build (and rebuild) the basilica, *palazzo*, and Campanile. The men who installed the first wooden piles underneath these buildings knew that they would never see them finished during their lifetimes. The Bellini restaurant four thousand miles west in the fair city of New York was a different story. I took notes during the ordeal. The following is taken from my diary of the time.

On the stroke of eight o'clock one Wednesday morning in March 1987, four metalworkers walked into the kitchen of a restaurant under construction in the Hotel Taft on Seventh Avenue. So in addition to the electricians, plumbers, and general workmen, now there were these four metalworkers.

Jerry was very young and very fat. He may have been strong but mostly he was flab, with a not-very-intelligent baby face. Tom had a beard. He was probably the brightest of the four, but he had no ideas of his own. He did what he was told. Timmy might have been forty, but he looked much older, with his gray hair and mustache and the watery eyes of a heavy smoker. He was the spitting image of Andy Capp. Barney could have been the down-on-his-luck maître d' of a Bronx brothel. He did absolutely nothing, but he was the boss.

That morning Barney said, "We've got to put up some shelves."

"Where are they?" Jerry asked.

"I think in those cardboard boxes," Barney answered.

"Let's check it out," said Tom. He picked up one of the boxes and started to remove the tape.

"They *look* like shelves," he said.

Barney asked, "Who's going for the coffee?"

"I'll go," Tom volunteered.

Everyone took out a dollar bill, and Barney counted each one carefully.

"Make mine with milk," said Barney.

They all sat down on the crates scattered around the kitchen. They talked about what they were going to do on the weekend. After all, it was already Wednesday.

Ten minutes later Tom came back with the coffee.

They lighted cigarettes and spent another ten minutes drinking coffee. By then it was almost nine o'clock.

"Come on, fellows, let's get these goddamn shelves up."

"How do they want them?" Jerry asked.

"What do you mean, how do they want them?"

"Three shelves high, four? Or maybe five?"

"Good question," Barney said.

"Better ask Frank," Timmy suggested.

"Anybody seen Frank?" Tom asked.

"No," the others replied, a New York chorus.

"Then we'll have to wait," said Barney. They sat down again on the crates and lighted cigarettes.

A half hour later Frank, the superintendent, came by.

"Hey," Barney yelled, "can you tell us how to put up these goddamn shelves?"

"The same way you always do," Frank answered.

"Very funny," said Barney. "We want to know how *many* shelves in each row."

"And how far off the floor do you want the bottom shelf, and how far down from the ceiling the top one," Jerry added.

"That's right," Barney nodded. "We wanna know how damn high we have to begin."

"Start a foot off the floor and finish a foot from the ceiling. Six shelves each," said Frank.

"Now you're talking," Barney said.

"Okay," said Frank, "get to work."

"What's the hurry? Is there a fire somewhere?" Timmy asked.

Frank wandered off, presumably to deal with his next major problem.

"I don't understand," Barney shook his head. "First they don't tell you a damn thing, then you have to do everything in a hurry. Okay, guys, let's unpack these damn shelves."

Tom finished tearing open the carton and pulled out three steel shelves and four corner posts. "There's only three shelves in here," he said.

"Maybe you need two boxes to make up one set of shelves," Jerry said, "but that'll mean four posts left over."

"Good thinking," said Barney. "We'd better ask Frank what to do. Tom, go see if you can find Frank."

They all sat back down on the crates.

"I don't like this job. There's nothing exciting about it," said Jerry.

"Jerry," Barney said, "look in another carton.

Maybe there's more than three shelves in one of these damn boxes."

Jerry tore open another box. "Nope," he said, "there are only three here, too."

"So we're screwed," said Barney. "We'll just have to wait for Frank."

A half hour later Frank came by.

"Why aren't the shelves up?" Frank said.

"Because if we put up six shelves each, we'll have four posts left over for each one."

"Doesn't matter," Frank said.

"These guys must have money to burn," Barney remarked.

"That's none of your business," Frank said.

"Just talking," Barney replied. "Okay, guys, let's get to work."

"It's almost noon," said Timmy. "We'd better knock off for lunch."

"Right," said Barney. "We'll finish the job after lunch."

All four went out to Seventh Avenue into the roar of traffic. Tom stopped to look at the gleaming gold watches a black man was hawking.

"What are you doing?" Barney asked.

"Looking at the watches," Tom replied. "They really look good!"

"They're fakes, for Christ's sake. Everybody knows that. C'mon!" Barney said.

They went into the café on the corner of Fifty-sixth Street and ordered hamburgers. While they ate, they continued talking about the shelving. An hour later they went back to the kitchen of the hopefully soon-to-be restaurant. Frank was waiting for them.

"There's a truck to unload," he said.

"A truckload of what?" Barney asked.

"Steel tables and a couple of ovens."

"Then you'll have to get two electricians as well," said Barney.

"They're already here," said Frank.

"Okay, guys," said Barney, "let's move it."

They went back out onto Seventh Avenue, and there was Sammy's truck.

Sammy was a young, very big Puerto Rican who owned his own truck; a nice white truck with enormous red letters on the side — THE GOLDEN SAMMY — surrounded by thousands of red stars.

"What's to unload?" Barney asked.

"Stuff that's probably too heavy for you weaklings," said Sammy.

They all laughed, but they weren't sure why.

Sammy got out and opened the rear door.

There was a bottle of Bacardi rum and a bottle of Pepsi-Cola in the corner. Sammy opened the rum and took a long swig. Then he took a sip of the Pepsi.

"Tomorrow is my big day," he said. "I'll be thirty!"

"What a coincidence!" exclaimed Barney, "tomorrow's my birthday too!"

"And your sister's, too," said Sammy. He swung the iron ramp down to the asphalt pavement.

"A table and two ovens," Sammy said.

"Let's take the table first," said Barney.

"That leaves us out," said one of the electricians, who had stopped what they were doing to be present at the unloading of the ovens.

"Go back to work," Timmy said. "We'll call you when we're ready with the ovens."

"Nice table," Jerry said caressing it. "Stainless steel. A real honey."

"Timmy," Barney said, "would you go get some coffee. That goddamn hamburger is giving me a royal pain in the gut."

While they waited for Timmy, they all sat down on the back of the truck dangling their legs.

Sammy kept on swigging from the two bottles.

A half hour went by, and there was no sign of Timmy.

"Jerry," Barney said, "go see what's happened to Timmy. All this smoking has given me a headache."

After a while Timmy arrived. There was a woman with him. She was about his age.

"Let me introduce my wife," Timmy said.

They all got down from the truck, quickly wiped their hands on the seat of their pants, and said, "Pleased to meet you."

"How do you manage to live with this guy?" Barney asked.

"We've been together twenty years," the woman replied. "I'm used to him by now."

"See?" Tom turned to Sammy, "you *can* get used to anything in life."

Sammy, drunk by now, nodded vacantly. He had trouble focusing on the men standing in front of him.

"Come on," he said, "we've got to get this truck unloaded. My wife is waiting for me at home."

"If that's all," said Timmy, "better to keep her waiting."

Sammy had difficulty climbing up on the truck. He started to move the table, and when he got it down the ramp to street level, the four metalworkers lifted it and carried it to the head of the stairs leading to the kitchen. Sammy followed them, swaying visibly.

"Hey," he shouted, "be careful on the stairs. That's valuable stuff!"

They stopped at the head of the stairs to decide whether to carry it right side up or upside down.

Jerry said it was better up. Tom insisted on turning it upside down. Barney said, "Let's get a nice big cardboard carton and slide it down."

"Good thinking," said Timmy. "I'll go find a carton."

"Go ask Frank," said Barney.

Timmy disappeared down the steps, and his wife said good-bye to the others.

"When'll you be home?" she yelled after Timmy.

"Can't you see how much there is to do!" he called up to her. "Not before eight."

Fifteen minutes later he was back with a large piece of cardboard.

"Good boy," said Barney.

They turned the table upside down and set it on the cardboard.

Timmy and Tom went down a few steps, and Sammy took hold of the two front legs.

"Okay, push the damn table." Tom shouted.

Sammy was sweating like a pig. He pushed the table toward the stairs, and when it was on the edge, Tom and Timmy gripped it from below and slowly moved backward, sliding it down step by step.

"Easy," said Barney, standing behind Sammy. "Don't hurt yourselves."

Sammy sat down on the top step and said: "I'll bet that damn table is worth a fortune."

A half hour later they all emerged from the kitchen.

"I need coffee before we get those ovens," Barney said. "I'll go this time."

It was two thirty. They were still standing at the back of the truck.

"We'll have to do overtime if we're ever going to finish," said Barney.

"Who's willing to stay?" he asked.

"I can't," said Tom.

"I can't either." Jerry wiped the sweat off his forehead. "I can only stay till three."

"Go call the electricians," Barney said.

Jerry came back in a while. "They said it's too

late now, and they can't do overtime either."

"That just leaves the two of us, me and Timmy," said Barney, "and the Puerto Rican drunk."

"Even drunk, I'm stronger than all you put together," said Sammy, staggering.

He got up on the truck and began to push the heavy oven all by himself.

"Hey, man!" Barney shouted. "Wait for us. You'll hurt yourself." One of them stood on the ramp, and the other climbed up on the truck.

Sammy got behind the oven and began to push with all his might until the oven tipped onto the ramp.

"Hold it," Timmy yelled. He had both hands on the oven and was ready to take it as it tipped onto the ramp. Barney joined him as Sammy gave it a last push.

"Careful," said Timmy. The oven weighed dangerously on his arms, and Barney's hands were weak. As boss, he wasn't used to this hard work. The oven started to slide down the ramp, and Timmy couldn't stop it by himself. Timmy and Barney were both yelling, and Sammy was laughing at the back of the truck. The oven gained speed and smashed onto the asphalt with a deafening thud.

Sammy stopped laughing. He eyed the disaster with a stupid smile. Barney and Timmy got an iron pipe to lever the dented oven up onto an oversized dolly. Then they pushed it to the door, edged it inside, and closed the door.

"Three o'clock," said Barney. "Time to quit."

"Damn right," Timmy said.

Sammy was in his truck. "Hey," he yelled, "what am I supposed to do with this other oven?"

"Bring it back tomorrow," Barney said. "Bright and early, okay? We start at eight sharp."

Sammy got back down from the truck, pulled up the ramp, and slammed the rear door shut. He scrambled into the cabin, started the engine, and with a belch and a hiccup the truck lurched forward. At Fiftieth Street, Sammy slumped over to the left, and the truck careened frighteningly around the corner.

I couldn't help thinking, as I watched my metalworkers knock off for the day: first, Did the builders of San Marco ever have days like this? and second, Was there a chance, however slim, that the Bellini would ever open?

15

THE SORT OF THINGS THAT HAPPEN IN NEW YORK

B<small>Y THIS TIME I HAD GOTTEN TO KNOW NEW YORK</small> almost as well as I knew Venice. From the start, I was taken by the energy and the personableness of New York, and I lent no credence to what I thought was its slanderous reputation as a dirty pit of vipers, with murderers and terrorists lurking around every corner. At first, I tried to be on my guard at all times, but my meditative nature soon got the better of me. This led me into some unexpected situations — all of which ultimately confirmed my opinion of New York as the most amazing metropolis outside of the Veneto.

About one o'clock in the morning one summer

Saturday, I went to get a quart of milk in one of those little New York stores that is open twenty-four hours a day, and I was approached by a shabbily dressed, very agitated black man with a happy-go-lucky face.

He waved his arms about wildly as he spoke. "Do me a favor, mister. My wife just took the Rolls and ran off with the chauffeur, and I haven't got the cash to get my Ferrari out of the parking lot. Give me a hand. I don't know what to do."

I was so astonished by his brilliant but unlikely story that, almost without realizing it, I put my hand in my pocket and pulled out a dollar a moment before the two very worried Thai clerks started weakly urging him out the door.

"Hey, hey!" he protested. "Don't you want my money? Nothing to buy here? This is good money!" And waving the dollar bill, he tried to resist. Meanwhile he kept winking in my direction until he was pushed outside.

I was still smiling as I took my quart of milk and stepped out to the street. He was still there. "Hey, mister!" he shouted. "You shouldn't buy anything in that store. They're so violent. There's too much violence. Too much violence, that's the trouble."

He went off down Third Avenue talking and waving his arms.

But after many years of frequent stays in the city, I still don't share his fear of violence. I often walk home from the restaurant at night. I don't live far away, maybe fifteen minutes at a leisurely pace, and I like walking. I have never witnessed any violence, nor have I ever sensed violence in the air. Quite the contrary. One evening my thoughts were elsewhere as I walked along, and I didn't see that I was headed straight at a man on the corner. He started waving his arms and shouting as I approached, "No, no!" I realized that for an instant he was afraid I was going to mug him. I was sorry to have frightened him, but I confess that I was also rather amused.

I sometimes wonder if there is more violence or more fear in New York. You can certainly feel uneasy in the presence of madness. At night, and especially in the summer, there are more male ghosts on the street than in other cities — sleeping ghosts, piles of rags with a man underneath. Or maybe a woman. Hopeless melancholy prisoners of the very street where they live. These harmless derelicts, almost always numb with liquor or drugs, frighten people. People are frightened to look at them, maybe frightened to understand them.

In the daytime, however, a lot of madmen save themselves from wisdom through outspoken disrespectful humor that is usually aimed at the powers that be. We used to have madmen in Venice too. For years there was a man who used to stand on the outer ramp of the Rialto Bridge in the evening. He would tunelessly scrape the strings of a rickety old guitar. No logical sound came out of it. Just to tease him, we children called him Segovia. "Let's hear it, Segovia," we would say. "Play us something." And he would laugh.

Then there was Adele, who always alternated invective with friendliness. Mario, the Number Man, could go on and on reciting increasingly gigantic numbers. Young Alfredo Oro, alias Pacéa, would walk along and every now and then suddenly emit a short hoarse shout. Eugenio was short of breath and couldn't carry a tune, but he held a page ripped out of an old music book against his cheek and sang. And then there is the nice, awful, and highly intelligent Praitano, who has fun terrifying passersby and people in bars with his looks and gestures.

Of course, New York has its own remarkable collection of eccentrics.

Louis Hanson is a Jamaican, and every evening at seven o'clock he sets up his street piano right outside our front door. He places an upturned cardboard box top on the pavement next to his instrument and looks around with a smile behind his graying mustache. His skin still preserves the Jamaican sun and rain after fifteen years in New York.

Every evening he plays the same song over and over again, very slowly picking out the hesitant keys with one finger. Those simple notes that seem to float above the deafening roar of Broadway strike me as unreal. Louis Hanson plays "Stardust" and smiles at everyone who gives him something: "God bless you," he calls after them as they head downtown. "You are a wonderful human being."

And every evening around eight o'clock I put a dollar in his pocket. And the restaurant is always miraculously full of people.

Then there was the suitcase incident.

It was sitting on the street in front of one of the two big windows looking out over Central Park. There was something a bit sinister about it sitting all alone in the middle of the wide pavement on Fifth Avenue. It seemed to have appeared out of nowhere. No one had noticed who put it or left it there. It was just past noon when the maître d' told me. "There's a suitcase outside the door," he said with that indifferent air Italian immigrants often acquire in America, as if it were no concern of his.

I went out at once to have a look. You couldn't help but notice it. It was a great big ugly old suitcase, and very dirty. It was made of colored cloth with a wide band of blue plastic down the middle. The zipper must have been forced shut, because the suitcase was packed full and heavy. No one dared to touch it. No one uttered the word "bomb," but that is what everyone thought it was. At least it looked more like a bomb than a suitcase. As soon as I saw it, I felt ill at ease. Everything else seemed to lose its usual liveliness, because that suitcase was so strangely immobile. I realized that I felt better looking at it straight on than when I turned my back. The minute I turned away, the skin under my hair started itching in a peculiar way. That must be what people mean when they talk about your hair standing on end.

The police arrived at twelve thirty, six cars with sirens off but yellow and white lights blinking on top. They drew up to the curb. A dozen policemen got out and stood in groups of three about fifty feet from the suitcase. I approached one group and asked if someone would be coming down to defuse it. They said the bomb squad was on its way, but the traffic was heavy and it would take them a while to get there.

I went back inside. The restaurant was full of people, but no one realized what was happening. Outside even passersby, whom the police did not try to stop, turned to give the suitcase an absent glance and continued on their way. Inside, two beautiful women sitting next to the window asked me what all the police were doing. I explained that there was a suitcase, and they asked to be moved to a table in the rear, away from the street. I moved them. Meanwhile more time passed, and still nothing happened. As I circulated among the tables, I wondered what would happen if the bomb went off. For a moment I could see it all in slow motion: the picture windows shattered into a million incandescent particles bursting through the dining room like a violent gust of wind, spreading panic and death.

It was a few minutes to one o'clock, and it occurred to me that if terrorists had put a timing device in the suitcase, they surely would have set it precisely for the hour. I went downstairs to the kitchen on the excuse that I had to speak to the cooks, but I came right back up, ashamed of myself for leaving my customers at the time of the explosion.

It was five minutes past one when I went back out to the street: I wanted to feel that strange sensation in my scalp again, and the closer I got to the suitcase the more my scalp tickled. My son was inside the door of the hotel next door, protected by a solid wall of jambs and doorposts, smiling and talking to the hotel manager. My son Giuseppe is very young and certainly wasn't ready to die so soon.

The policemen seemed to be getting nervous, and they all eyed the bomb. It was about one thirty when another police car pulled up. A man in uniform got out, calmly went up to the suitcase, and knelt down beside it. He took a very sharp little knife and cut a round hole in the fabric. He pointed his flashlight and looked warily inside the suitcase. He delicately drew out a rag and put it on the pavement next to him, and then another and several more after that. Soon there was a pile of rags on the sidewalk on one side of the policeman and a deflated suitcase on the other. Then he stood up, got into his car, and went off. And immediately the other policemen all left too. A cleaning man came out of the hotel with a broom and dustpan to sweep up the useless remains of the suitcase.

One afternoon a couple of days later, I was standing in the middle of the packed restaurant when an odd smell almost unconsciously turned my nose in the air. I sniffed and noticed that the maître d' and the waiters were doing the same thing. I looked out the big window to see what was happening on Fifth Avenue and heard the sound of a parade. It was then that I realized the smell we had all noticed came from the hot-dog wagon parked outside our restaurant. We all laughed.

On days like this Fifth Avenue is full of people. There are so many people on the street, it looks as if the natural order of things might be upset. Manhattan is an assemblage of people and traffic lights, and the traffic lights are there to regulate the people. Except that when so many people are out walking, the street corners seem swamped by a tender and impatient violence. The automobiles always win but not by much.

I went outside and was immediately enveloped by the festive blare of trumpets and drums. I don't know what parade it was, one of the many that begin down toward Forty-sixth Street and come up Fifth Avenue along Central Park as far as Ninetieth Street. It might have been the Irish or the Chinese who were parading, or the Italians or the bicyclists. Not that it matters, they're all alike. On the other side of the pointless barriers the police hurriedly erect in the morning, there are usually a great many vibrant majorette legs, groups of very serious pathetic war veterans, various bands playing to a vaguely martial beat, and, always, a sweet and noisy atmosphere like a rural *festa* in Italy.

That is how it was that morning, too. I smiled at the hot-dog man, and casually mentioned that at least half of the sweetish blue effluvium of his wursts was coming into the restaurant. He responded with an understanding smile, one colleague to another. He pushed the electric button of his pushcart and moved it a few yards up the wide pavement in the direction of the parade. Soon the windswept smoke was cheerily profaning the august foyer of the Hotel Pierre.

Then there is of course New York's underworld, the world of the subway and the deafening sound of steel as the trains run underground. It still fascinates me. People on the subway seem numb and resigned, but occasionally a miracle happens. The other day, I was hanging on a metal strap, and I thought I heard a child's light singsong voice. I turned and saw a black woman slowly advancing from the other end of the car. She was very fat and wore a long threadbare purple dress down to her feet. The hollows of her blind eyes stared lifelessly up into infinite darkness.

She held a very long thin white cane in one hand, her left one, and she tapped it lightly from side to side. She held a little tin cup, like a milk pot, between two fingers of her right hand. She moved slowly but always kept her incredible balance on the storm-tossed floor of the car. Meanwhile she was singing. It wasn't even a song, just a tuneless hum in a very faint voice, but a voice that was clear and slender, as slender as a silk thread that might suddenly snap.

It was only when she was very close that I could hear the words and recognize the song that repeated ad infinitum: "Baby my love . . . baby my love." And as she walked on, setting one foot down after the other with the calm of ages past, the miracle happened. All the men and women in the car put a coin in the woman's cup. They did it very carefully and almost furtively so as not to disturb her progress or interrupt the song, which she was still repeating when I got off the train at my stop. And for a long time afterward the words continued in my head, "Baby my love . . . baby my love."

16

AGAINST FOOD INTERPRETATION

A SUBSTANTIAL PART OF THE POPULATION of Manhattan and its environs — for a host of reasons that generally have nothing whatsoever to do with what a customer ought to expect of a restaurant — believes the words of fairly well known food columnists with the same faith that Christians have in the Bible and Moslems in the Koran.

That kind of reader devotion, I imagine, is also the secret dream of some Italian journalists who are more familiar with gastritis than they are with gastronomy, but, fortunately, Italians are able to read between the lines thanks to the lens of providence's gift to our nation, its sense of humor.

I remember a time when the fearsome critic of the *New York Times* came to try our food and drink. The news that he was in the restaurant spread via winks and discreet thumb-pointing in the direction of his table. I immediately instructed the waiters to pretend he was not there. Everyone should do the usual things and act as if they had never seen him before. The famous food critic ought to be served and treated just like any other customer. He was seated with a friend, and they had ordered risotto and carpaccio.

That news was also relayed at once. We all sighed with relief. It was an easy order, we were fully armed with risotto and carpaccio. But I was worried about the way he looked. He looked more like a bookkeeper than someone who tasted food from morning till night. He was as thin as a rail and wore thick-lensed tortoiseshell glasses.

You see, my idea is that the ideal gastronome ought to be a fat man, with a reassuring air of opulence, a hearty appetite, and an inclination to laughter and forgiveness. Instead the critic looked like a special envoy from a company board of directors sent round to check the books. Yet there he was preparing, with the detachment and attention to minute detail of a pathologist, to analyze the sophisticated secrets, the hard-won recondite flavors, the subtle refinements, and the veiled whispers of my dishes, the quality of the butter, the correct gestures of the service, the temperature of the containers, the erotic and tremulous consistency of the béchamel, and the hidden truth of the Brix index of our sorbets.

AGAINST FOOD INTERPRETATION

I assigned two trusted waiters to serve him, two
men who could transfer a risotto from an ovenproof dish
to the plate and set it down delicately without compro-
mising its soft elegance, and do so in constant awareness
of the work of all the men and women who had helped
bring it to the table, including the backbreaking work of
the women who had planted the rice and the perspiring,
anxious care of the farmer who'd tended its growth. Attention to every detail, just the way we were taught by
Madame Valentina Schlee, renowned designer.

A reassuring calm prevailed in the kitchen. Chef
Nicola lowered his lids and said: "Rest easy!" while the
French cook Philippe was vigorously and lovingly mixing the semirefined grains of dwarf rice that were taking
on the golden color of the lightly sautéed fresh onion.
And the American Bruce was preparing the filet for the
carpaccio.

When the famous food critic was served, he sat for
a moment in careful observation of all the points of form.
I saw his nostrils dilate as he breathed in the aroma. With
the expressionless mien of a great poker player, he took
the fork and held it delicately. Then with a light gesture
he skillfully slid some of the risotto on the tines of his
fork and brought it to his mouth.

I trembled as I saw all the waiters stop and look,
the way a herd of African gnus stop to watch a lion that
suddenly appears on the crest of a distant hill. The famous journalist whispered something to his companion,
and the two of them nodded. Disaster. At a distance I
could read their lips. He'd whispered: "Salt."

171

I believe that cooking is in real danger. Cooking in the past twenty years has often seen cerebral onanism take the place of healthy masturbation. The preachers of this new route to "pleasure" are food writers who work off their frustrations by waging war against hated tradition.

The danger first appeared in the early seventies, after the revolution of 1968, which, it is common knowledge, was not fostered by poverty or social inequity but by well-being. This totally unlikely event also struck cooking via the rejection of all the ways food was prepared in the past. There was a total lack of humility and of any understanding of man's history, customs, and needs; and under the banner of the pure and the genuine, cooking all but stopped.

Without the essential component, namely flavor, the art of cooking has in recent years turned into a glorification of image. Indeed, cooking in the 1970s produced a host of painters and many sculptors, but very few cooks. Sauces were banned, except — who knows why — for cream sauces, and the pursuit of poor, undercooked food was fostered as a natural reaction against any dangerous signs of opulence. The results were negative acculturation, total loss of content, and pseudoecological dietetics. A real trump of snobbery. Equality in mediocrity in a so-called free form.

The authors of the gospels of gastronomy swooned in delirium over the "new" and over "angels at table" as they tried to elevate the soul of the poor "bourgeois" accustomed solely to the humble level of the neighborhood diner.

Now the poor fool was forced to contemplate and eat petals from heaven. He was made to believe that he was close to paradise. A very great deal of responsibility for this state of affairs is also due to the big hotel chains that were being taken over by rampant financiers and bookkeepers. Jimmy Sherwood's lesson was taken to heart.

Until 1960, hotels, especially luxury hotels, set the standard for service and cooking. I do not claim that the results were always stirring, but the hotel chefs were meticulous teachers and carried forward the tradition that was the foundation of great cooking in the first half of this century.

In the 1970s service was replaced by service management. The guest of a luxury hotel, the nameless client, was obliged to read written communiqués from the hotel office and be kind enough to complete a written questionnaire before checking out. A true scandal.

In an attempt to be both brief and optimistic, I shall say only that at least two things are starting to become clear. One, people are beginning to be fed up with eating in the stern company of the angels; and two, man, to our great good fortune, is and remains a sinner. So I foresee a wish to return to tradition, a longing for quite human opulence, and an almost irresistible mania to free the tongue from its condom and once again taste the flavor of friendly foods.

It seems to me that the time is ripe to bring real cooks back to the stove. There will be a new revolution. The exact opposite of the other. The revolution of the eater. For my part, I seriously suggest we begin by beheading Gault and Millau and their ilk, bombing the refrigerator bar, tossing service communiqués into the fire, and confiscating the hotel-chain hotels and turning them over to dirt farmers. The future of cooking, and the future of the world, ought to be back in the hands of human beings.

17

EXCERPTS FROM THE SUGGESTIONS BOX

Valerio Zurlini, the eminent filmmaker, had been ill for a long time before he died in 1982, but what shocked him half to death was being president of the jury at the Venice Film Festival that year. He could not bear the idea that Fassbinder had won the prize for a film Zurlini considered incomprehensible, so remote from the lightness of his own spiritual being.

I don't know where to begin to describe him. He was an extremely talented director. A man of letters. A poet. And he loved Venice meltingly. But if I had to choose a single word that fit him best, it would be *sensitive*. He was a delicate, clean, fragile, and strong man.

One of those whose loss you really feel after they are gone.

He rented an apartment in Venice and was often at Harry's Bar. It was like home to him.

One day Zurlini came as usual before noon for a martini and handed me a letter on his way out.

"Read it, Cipriani," he said, "and then do what you like with it."

As soon as I finished reading his letter, I took pen in hand and replied at once. But I wanted to enjoy his reaction firsthand, so, instead of mailing it, I handed it to him a few days later at Harry's Bar. It was early evening and the place was full. He opened the letter at once and began to read it before sitting down.

I watched in curiosity from behind the bar counter, where I all but hid to have a leisurely view. I was deliberately stern in the first part of the letter, so that it would take a while before he realized it was all a joke. As soon as he began reading, his face turned serious and concerned. He really believed that I had been offended by his letter. Tears actually seemed to well up in his eyes. It seemed incredible to him that I had failed to understand that *his* letter was a joke. By the time he reached the part about Count Temistocle's spaghetti, however, he understood. At that point he raised his head and looked around for me. He rushed over and embraced me. Then he laughed. "Arrigo," he said, "you are going to be very sorry you wrote this!"

Two days later he opened the door to Harry's Bar

and tossed another letter on the bar counter. I decided to publish the exchange of letters that ensued, to the immense delight of both of us. Then came the Venice Film Festival, and then he fell badly ill. He sent his son to deliver his last short poem, and I replied in kind.

Wednesday, March 10, 1982

Dear Arrigo Cipriani,

This short letter is totally platonic, because, anticipating the "nefarious" response you threatened, I might as well tell you at once that I will never stop coming to Harry's Bar, even if you were to double your already exorbitant prices just for me. I consider it my true home in Venice, and I regret only that I do not enjoy the income of Signor Bagnasco, whom you like even less than me, or the wealth that was Paul Getty's. Otherwise I would simply move in permanently, from morning coffee to the last nightcap.

Indeed, you open too late in the morning for my taste.

Yet I am obliged to come around ever less frequently: I order three glasses of wine and a sandwich. I do all I can to avoid the place, except when irrepressible fondness for the way I am treated forces me to say, especially this year: "So what, I'll just go deeper into debt."

I have not collected the signatures of people who make this honorable offer, but when I have I swear there won't be more than six (or seven).

But we are all people who — one way or another,

in poverty or in days of splendor — have each added a brick to your (our) house. Which is why I ask you to meet us halfway, in part to avoid having to provide for me in depressing old age. Moreover, my friends and I have always paid our tabs, and you can testify to that — except for the last bill, and that for reasons of superstition.

Well then, I do not care how nefarious your response is, I will still be at Harry's Bar tomorrow morning.

Your old and devoted friend,

Valerio Zurlini

Friday, March 12

Dear Mr. Zurlini,

Today I received your letter of March 10, and although you kindly warned me in advance of its contents, I confess it has left me feeling very grieved. I have always thought that our work needed constant feedback through the criticism of our customers, but at the same time I believe that the great constancy of the efforts we all make should be given fair consideration, even when our work — which, I assure you, is always aimed at continuous improvement — does not seem to some people to achieve the desired result.

Which is exactly what seems to have happened on the present occasion.

It grieves me all the more when I think of so many

other events in the fifty years we have been in business, events that have prompted altogether different judgments.

I can quote, just as an example, the exemplary behavior, the gentlemanly neglect, and the courteous remark of a devoted customer, Count Temistocle, who in 1953 had the misfortune of being the protagonist of the great *taglierini al pomodoro* disaster. To make a long story short, his white dinner jacket was ruined by the seventy pounds of *taglierini al pomodoro* a distracted waiter spilled on him as he was dining with the great actress Tatiana. Despite everything, he continued to sing the praises of our service.

Instead I read between the lines of your letter, which I certainly cannot call courteous, remarks that constantly refer to prices as "terribly exorbitant" and complaints about when we open, which you say is "too late." Also between the lines, it is not hard to perceive implicit criticism of the quality of our wine and our superb sandwiches, as if they were the last remains of leftover food!

All of this sugared by a "Harry's is my home," when, instead, it is common knowledge in the Salute quarter that you are becoming an increasingly assiduous habitué of the Cantinone Storico! And yet you ask for benevolent consideration so that we will not have to look after your depressing old age. Allow me to say that you haven't the least consideration for all we do every day, racking body and mind, and just to please you. Indeed! We import scampi from distant Dalmatia, and I remember full well what happened the day there were no scampi! You have to admit that I am right about this too. We grow rice in the paddies that were dear to Virgil, and butter is creamed off the milk of impetuous cows of Swiss descent.

In any case, that is always the saloonkeeper's bitter fate, as my father used to say.

I have forwarded your letter for consideration by the board of directors, which will be meeting in the next few days. I make no promises. In spite of everything I shall try to defend your wishes in all their venality.

Yours,

Arrigo Cipriani

Sunday, March 14

Mr. Cipriani,

Never, for any reason, could I have expected a reply to my courteous letter that was as arrogant, malicious, and overbearing as yours. Mind you, I refrain from saying "outrageous." And the matter of Count Temistocle is none of my affair. You failed to give his surname, but I am quite familiar with it, and subsequent to the notorious misfortune, which I would never have mentioned, he had sixty-seven new dinner jackets in different shades of white custom-made by Ciro Giuliano, the tailor (81 Corso Italia, Rome; telephone: 871-3927), which he made a point of never paying for. But that is none of my business. Nor am I acquainted with Tatiana the actress (could it be Pavlova?).

Your prices — despite your dignified manage-

ment and a thoroughly respectable, or at least respectful, past — are terribly exorbitant, and people never
cease to complain about them throughout the lagoon.
But I invite you totally to ignore the letter I mistakenly
wrote you, perhaps in a moment of depression due to
my current poverty, and I do not blame you even for
my advanced state of cirrhosis due to the martinis that
you have been mixing for thirty years without an ounce
of pity.

You tendentiously refer to my veiled complaints
about the quality of your food and carafe wine, which I
have never ever deplored. The Cantinone Storico has
become a benevolent and fragile harbor for me because
of our nation's well-known difficulty with the current
exchange rate of the dollar. You, not I, are the one who
spoke of the last remains of leftovers in the sandwiches
(perhaps a guilty conscience? I do not know), and
henceforth you can set them out on the last beach-
head for American sailors, your summer habitués who,
marked for disaster, will soon be landing in Cuba and
Nicaragua.

The unnamed fans to whom you make perfidious allusions may have ducal maces in their bed-
side tables, while the present writer is a patrician of
Parma, a nobleman of the Holy Roman Empire (see
the *Golden Book of Italian Noblemen*, last edition 1947,
published by Poligrafico dello Stato, 2 Piazza Verdi,
Rome), who — out of gentlemanly modesty and dem-
ocratic reserve — only displays his academic titles (in
which regard, professor, not merely doctor).

Your scampi may well come from Dalmatia, I in-
sinuate nothing, but you might look for them closer

to home, to Chioggia or San Benedetto del Tronto, not to mention the Lofoten islands. Your fish is fresh, that I will grant. Moreover, on principle and by natural inclination, I eschew denigration, I never referred to your place as a saloon, though you refer to yourself as a saloonkeeper. The rice paddies are not farmed by you, as you would suggest, but by the Curti Company, a dignified and prosperous business that has never been known to export cat excrement in the form of Modena *mortadella*. And as for those Swiss cows, who can tell?

Valerio Zurlini

P.S. I am sending this letter to your home address to spare you the embarrassment of blushing in front of your staff for the shameful way you have treated me.

Tuesday, March 16

Dear Professor,

Thank you for writing again and giving me the opportunity to confirm that my judgment of you was not erroneous. I do not think I owe you any reply, but I noted between your lines a host of inexactitudes and misinformation that demand some correction on my part.

First: the dinner jackets that the tailor Giuliano made for Count Temistocle were regularly paid for by Lloyd's of London, with whom we are insured. It is common knowledge (which seems to have escaped your notice), because the bell in the City of London that usually tolls news of shipwrecks rang out that day.

And another thing. Let me direct your attention

to page 47 of the same edition of the *Golden Book* that you so pompously quote to remind me of your noble descent. There you will find that Cangrande della Scala was able to sate his unbridled thirst for conquest only thanks to loans from an obscure Veronese banker named Cipriani, who earned no honor from that, nor was he even repaid, for which reason he went bankrupt, and all of us Ciprianis are still suffering the consequences.

Some years later, my maternal grandfather, a Socialist switchman for the Italian state railway in the days before Craxi (responsible for switching the *rapido* trains at the Porta Vescovo station in Verona; and in forty years of service, he had only one train derailed with thirty-five injured), a grandfather from whom I inherited some social conscience as well as a troublesome prostate; and my paternal grandfather, a small manufacturer of toothpicks (he made them by hand, lined them up neatly in the band of his broad hat, and sold them outside restaurants) — as I was saying, some years later, one of these grandfathers conceived my mother and the other my father, and those two, together, brought me into this world, as they say, for the following reason, among others: to demand repayment from the noble houses of Italy of that debt incurred by the Veronese conqueror.

You see how it is, it is better not to mention things that are not common knowledge. In any event, you do not realize that I had taken a liking to you and tried to do everything possible to make you spend all the money you had, so that you could in time become a customer of the famous tavern where I intend to spend

183

the last ten years of my business life. Keep your money, because you will never set foot in my tavern! The food will be very good in that tavern, and, what is more, the prices will be very low!

Unless you decide to write me not just an apology but an act of total submission, I see no future for you.

Yours truly,

Arrigo Cipriani

Thursday, March 23

Dear Cipriani,

What on earth has happened? I received two other letters together with yours, which I will discuss later. One is signed "Quite unlikely employees" and the other is from your cashier. Both letters describe you as a cruel-hearted person capable of anything. I cannot believe it!

True, there was a torturer named Cipriani at Bergen-Belsen (you know I have a weakness for history), but my investigations have shown this to be a false homonym. It was a certain Cipriansky, a Bohemian of Ruthenian descent, and he ended up before a firing squad at Mazara del Vallo after six hours commanding the famous Tartar SS battalion Azimov-Sokolimovsky.

Between us, and I ask you to keep this letter secret, I admit that what I am sure is totally unfounded anxiety on the part of the cashier may have been dictated by a passing and fragile bond (granted, a senile bond) fostered by her kindness when I had to pay the bill.

This bond — I swear by my honor that there was nothing the least bit felonious — never went beyond the platonic limit of glances, of one — I repeat, one — caress on the little finger of her left hand, and perhaps some slight clandestine discount. But the fact remains that women are impetuous and passionate creatures, and if they do not or cannot give themselves, they delete service and cover charges. I ask you not to take any action against her, and I declare my readiness to repay the slight differences.

Why submission? When did I ever offend you at all? I cannot think. Or did someone misuse my name or, why not, my letterhead? (Check the filigree: Fabriano thirteenth century, the most expensive paper on the market.)

But let us turn to your latest letter, which is incomprehensible and enigmatic, albeit as polite as ever.

I have nothing to say about Cangrande della Scala, who may have cheated on some gold coins, but such was the grand custom of the time. But with the speed of lightning (see above), I looked into the matter of your Cipriani grandfather, a pre-Craxi Socialist switchman.

In the matter of your paternal grandfather, let me inform you that he was known as an unrepentant brawling drunk; that the railway disaster of February 6, 1918, caused by an excess of delirium tremens resulted not in 35 injured but in 350 dead. (Ah, those zeros, if only you removed them from your bills as you do from your family's black book!)

I go on at length just for the pleasure of rambling: that should give you some idea of how far I am from understanding the meaning of your missive. (Have you been sipping a bit of Cartizze, my dear Cipriani?)

You speak of long periods of scanty rations to consolidate the family fortune, but that was long, long ago, come now! Your present guests (I have never had the honor of being among the privileged few) report that dishes are served at your table that would be worthy of Stalin or the Sun King, such as fried lilies, magnolia profiteroles, virgin sweat soufflé, and gigot of Kenya rhinoceros.

As to your new tavern (surely Ye Taverne), you will have to agree that if it is a public place, no one can forbid me to enter.

I pay in cash or, at worst, with an expired American Express card or rubber checks, but what does that matter, since my signature is familiar and dear to you?

So why did I bother to answer you? There has been no correspondence between us, but it was my pleasure to have a chat with you without a trace of submission.

Your devoted,

Valerio Zurlini

Monday, March 27

Dear Mr. Zurlini,

Forgive me for taking so long to reply to your letter of March 10. What I am about to tell you is quite incred-

ible. In truth I still do not understand. The tone of the
two letters you wrote after your first one and the odd
way you have behaved these past days — behavior that
I simply cataloged as another one of the passing odd-
ities of some of our customers — convinced me that
something very serious must have happened.

I have your letter of March 10 before me, a sweet
letter, so polite and full of kind words, however
undeserved, about the quality of our place, as well as
touching observations, dictated not by sentimentality
but by true affection. It is witty and full of humorous banter and exquisite double meanings, and it ends
with a polite and gentlemanly request for "special attention," which I will be glad to offer you always, absolutely always. Then I look at your second letter (dated
March 14), which is alarming from the outset. There is
a change from "Dear Arrigo Cipriani" in the first letter
to "Mr. Cipriani" in the second; and still more alarming, it speaks of the arrogant, malicious, and haughty
reply I am accused of making to your first letter.

Please believe me, Mr. Zurlini, it is a bolt from
the blue. How could you possibly fail to understand at
once that you had received a forgery! What surprises
me a bit is your immediate reaction, which was so hard
and so malicious. It suggests, if you will forgive me
for saying so, that your cordial sentiment is something
more fragile than a calm and consolidated fondness. All
I can do is register the fact, even imagining the most
atrocious and nefarious response on your part, that your
admiration crumbled at a few words of doubtful origin.
All you needed to do was telephone!

And then there is the third letter. And here I ask

you urgently to send me those apocryphal documents for my edification. You leap from talk about Bergen-Belsen to Azimov Cipriansky. There are only two possible explanations: either you suddenly went mad or you did not realize, and this is the simple truth, that the person who wrote to you was demented. I notice one little, almost insignificant confession that troubles me, namely your secret liaison with the cashier, a relationship that you call platonic. I do not see how you can use that term when your secret "union" involves sleight of hand and, if you will allow me, sleight of money — money that, failing evidence to the contrary, is mine.

Let that suffice. This time I shall deliver "my" letter by hand. I cannot beg your pardon for what I have not done or written. But I can tell you that I consider you one of the few rare "masters" I have had the good fortune to meet.

Yours,

Arrigo Cipriani